Great
Temple
of
For
Deadlands

Sef

Ye'dai
Forest

Channel of
Sad'hidyx

Coldulek

Tuerghaxug

rt Deso

Port Maien

Quadlara

Sendhi

Pass
of Torla

Cornaliant

Dostal

Hera

Torgai
Mountains

MAPS AND LEGENDS

READING AND WRITING ALONG THE BORDERLANDS

MICHAEL CHABON

5/08

McSWEENEY'S BOOKS

SAN FRANCISCO

www.mcsweeneys.net

ISBN: 978-1-932416-89-3

To Ayelet

ACKNOWLEDGMENTS

	1	2	3	4	5	6	7
A							
B							
C							
D							

 INSPIRATION   EDITING

OPPORTUNITY   HELP

Andelman........... C-4   Dario .... D-6   Kennison C-1

Arana .... C-1   Eggers .... B-6   Mendelsohn A-6

S Barclay .... C-3   L Eglington .... D-6   Rouse B-5

N Barruci .... C-4   Evans .... D-6   Schutz C-4

Barth .... A-5   E Frank .... C-1   Silvers C-1

E Napoleon .... B-5   Hederman .... C-4   Waldman........... B-5

Chaykin............. D-7   E Horowitz........ B-6

D'Aulaires .... C-1   Katchor D-7

The more I dive into this matter of whaling, and push my researches up to the very spring-head of it, so much the more am I impressed with its great honorableness and antiquity; and especially when I find so many great demi-gods and heroes, prophets of all sorts, who one way or other have shed distinction upon it, I am transported with the reflection that I myself belong, though but subordinately, to so emblazoned a fraternity.

—Herman Melville, on the writing of fan fiction

TABLE OF CONTENTS

Also by Michael Chabon

THE AMAZING ADVENTURES OF KAVALIER & CLAY
A MODEL WORLD AND OTHER STORIES
THE YIDDISH POLICEMEN'S UNION
THE MYSTERIES OF PITTSBURGH
WEREWOLVES IN THEIR YOUTH
GENTLEMEN OF THE ROAD
THE FINAL SOLUTION
WONDER BOYS
SUMMERLAND

MAPS AND LEGENDS

TRICKSTER IN A SUIT OF LIGHTS
THOUGHTS ON THE MODERN SHORT STORY

E NTERTAINMENT HAS A bad name. Serious people learn to mistrust and even to revile it. The word wears spandex, pasties, a leisure suit studded with blinking lights. It gives off a whiff of Coppertone and dripping Creamsicle, the fake-butter miasma of a movie-house lobby, of karaoke and Jägermeister, Jerry Bruckheimer movies, a *Street Fighter* machine grunting solipsistically in a corner of an ice-rink arcade. Entertainment trades in cliché and product placement. It engages regions of the brain far from the centers of discernment, critical thinking, ontological speculation. It skirts the black heart of life and drowns life's lambency in a halogen glare. Intelligent people must keep a certain distance from its productions. They must handle the things that entertain them with gloves of irony and postmodern tongs. Entertainment, in short, means junk, and too much junk is bad for you—bad for your heart, your arteries, your mind, your soul.

But maybe these intelligent and serious people, my faithful straw men, are wrong. Maybe the reason for the junkiness of so much of what pretends to entertain us is that we have accepted—indeed, we have helped to articulate—such a narrow, debased concept of entertainment. The brain is an organ of entertainment, sensitive at any depth, and over a wide spectrum. But we have learned to mistrust and despise our human aptitude for being entertained, and in that sense we get the entertainment we deserve.

I'd like to believe that, because I read for entertainment, and I write to entertain. Period. Oh, I could decoct a brew of other, more impressive motivations and explanations. I could uncork some stuff about reader response theory, or the Lacanian *parole*. I could go on about the storytelling impulse and the need to make sense of experience through story. A spritz of Jung might scent the air. I could adduce Kafka's formula: "A book must be an ice-axe to break the seas frozen inside our soul." I could go down to the café at the local mega-bookstore and take some wise words of Abelard or Koestler about the power of literature off a mug. But in the end—here's my point—it would still all boil down to *entertainment*, and its suave henchman, pleasure. Because when the axe bites the ice, you feel an answering throb of delight all the way from your hands to your shoulders, and the blade tolls like a bell for miles.

Therefore I would like to propose expanding our definition of entertainment to encompass everything pleasurable that arises from the encounter of an attentive mind with a page of literature.

Here is a sample, chosen at random from my career as a reader, of encounters that would be covered under my new definition of entertainment: the engagement of the interior ear by the rhythm and pitch of a fine prose style; the dawning awareness that giant mutant rat people dwell in the walls of a ruined abbey in England;

two hours spent bushwhacking through a densely packed argument about the structures of power as embodied in nineteenth-century prison architecture; the consummation of a great love aboard a lost Amazon riverboat, or in Elizabethan slang; the intricate fractal patterning of motif and metaphor in Nabokov and Neil Gaiman's *Sandman*; stories of pirates, zeppelins, sinister children; a thousand-word-long sentence comparing homosexuals to the Jews in a page of Proust (vol. 3); a duel to the death with broadswords on the seacoast of ancient Zingara; the outrageousness of whale slaughter or human slaughter in Melville or McCarthy; the outrageousness of Dr. Charles Bovary's clubfoot-correcting device; the outrageousness of outrage in a page of Philip Roth; words written in smoke across the sky of London on a day in June 1923; a momentary gain in one's own sense of shared despair, shared nullity, shared rapture, shared loneliness, shared broken-hearted glee; the recounting of a portentous birth, a disastrous wedding, or a midnight deathwatch on the Neva.

The original sense of the word "entertainment" is a lovely one of mutual support through intertwining, like a pair of trees grown together, interwoven, each sustaining and bearing up the other. It suggests a kind of midair transfer of strength, contact across a void, like the tangling of cable and steel between two lonely bridgeheads. I can't think of a better approximation of the relation between reader and writer. Derived senses of fruitful exchange, of reciprocal sustenance, of welcome offered, of grasp and interrelationship, of a slender span of bilateral attention along which things are given and received, still animate the word in its verb form: we entertain visitors, guests, ideas, prospects, theories, doubts, and grudges.

At some point, inevitably, as generations of hosts entertained generations of guests with banquets and feasts and displays of artifice, the idea of pleasure seeped into the pores of the word. And along with pleasure (just as inevitably, I suppose) came disapproval, a sense of hollowness and hangover, the saturnine doubtfulness that attaches to delight and artifice and show: to pleasure, that ambiguous gift. It's partly the doubtfulness of pleasure that taints the name of entertainment. Pleasure is unreliable and transient. Pleasure is Lucy with the football. Pleasure is easily synthesized, mass-produced, individually wrapped. Its benefits do not endure, and so we come to mistrust them, or our taste for them.

The other taint is that of passivity. At some point in its history, the idea of entertainment lost its sense of mutuality, of exchange. One either entertains or is entertained, is the actor or the fan. As with all one-way relationships, grave imbalances accrue. The entertainer balloons with a dangerous need for approval, validation, love, and box office; while the one entertained sinks into a passive spectatorship, vacantly munching great big salty handfuls right from the foil bag. We can't take pleasure in a work of art, not in good conscience, without accepting the implicit intention of the artist to please us. But somewhere along the course of the past century or so, as the great machinery of pleasure came online, turning out products that, however pleasurable, suffer increasingly from the ills of mass manufacture— spurious innovation, inferior materials, alienated labor, and an excess of market research—that intention came to seem suspect, unworthy, and somehow cold and hungry at its core, like the eyes of a brilliant comedian. Lunch counters, muffler shops, dinner theaters, they aim to please; but *writers?* No self-respecting literary genius, even an occasional maker of avowed entertainments like Graham Greene, would ever describe him- or herself as primarily an "entertainer." An entertainer is a man in a sequined dinner jacket, singing "She's a Lady" to a hall filled with women rubber-banding their underpants up onto the stage.

Yet entertainment—as I define it, pleasure and all—remains the only sure means we have of bridging, or at least of feeling as if we have bridged, the gulf of consciousness that separates each of us from everybody else. The best response to those who would cheapen and exploit it is not to disparage or repudiate but to reclaim entertainment as a job fit for artists and for audiences, a two-way exchange of attention, experience, and the universal hunger for connection.

Of all the means writers of fiction have devised for spanning the chasm between two human skulls, the short story maps the most efficient path. Cartographers employ different types of maps—political, topographic, dot—to emphasize different kinds of information. These different types are complementary; taken together they increase our understanding. I would like to argue for the common-sense proposition that, in constructing our fictional maps as short-story writers, we are foolish to restrict ourselves to one type or category.

Imagine that, sometime about 1950, it had been decided, collectively, informally, a little at a time, but with finality, to proscribe every kind of novel but the nurse romance from the canon of the future. Not merely from the critical canon, but from the store racks and library shelves as well. Nobody could be paid, published, lionized, or cherished among the gods of literature for writing any kind of fiction other than nurse romances. Now, because of my faith and pride in the diverse and rigorous brilliance of American writers of the last half century, I do believe that from this bizarre decision, in this theoretical

America, a dozen or more authentic masterpieces would have emerged. Thomas Pynchon's *Blitz Nurse*, for example, and Cynthia Ozick's *Ruth Puttermesser, R.N.* One imagines, however, that this particular genre—that any genre, even one far less circumscribed in its elements and possibilities than the nurse romance—would have paled somewhat by now. In that oddly diminished world, somebody, somewhere, is laying down his copy of *Dr. Kavalier & Nurse Clay* with a weary sigh.

Instead of "the novel" and "the nurse romance," try this little thought experiment with "jazz" and "the bossanova," or with "cinema" and "fish-out-of-water comedies." Now go ahead and try it with "short fiction" and "the contemporary, quotidian, plotless, moment-of-truth revelatory story."

Suddenly you find yourself sitting right back in your very own universe.

Okay, I confess. I am that bored reader, in that circumscribed world, laying aside his book with a sigh; and the book is my own, and it is filled with my own short stories, plotless and sparkling with epiphanic dew. It was in large part a result of a crisis in my own attitude toward my work in the short-story form that sent me back into the stream of alternate time, back to the world as it was before we all made that fateful and perverse decision.

As late as about 1950, if you referred to "short fiction," you might have been talking about any one of the following kinds of stories: the ghost story; the horror story; the detective story; the story of suspense, terror, fantasy, science fiction, or the macabre; the sea, adventure, spy, war, or historical story; the romance story. All these genres and others have rich traditions in America, reaching straight back to Poe and Hawthorne, our first great practitioners of the form. A glance at any dusty paperback anthology of classic tales turns up important genre work by

Balzac, Wharton, Conrad, Graves, Maugham, Faulkner, Twain, Cheever, Coppard. Heavyweights all, some considered among the giants of modernism, the very source of the moment-of-truth story that, like Homo sapiens, appeared relatively late on the scene but has worked very quickly to wipe out all its rivals. One of the pioneers of the modern "psychological" short story as we now generally understand it, Henry James (famously derided by critic Maxwell Geismar as merely "a major entertainer"), wrote so many out-and-out ghost stories that they fill an entire book. "Genre" short stories were published not only by the unabashedly entertaining pulps, which gave us Hammett, Chandler, and Lovecraft among a very few other writers now enshrined more or less safely in the canon, but also in the great "slick" magazines of the time: the *Saturday Evening Post*, *Esquire*, *Collier's*, *Liberty*, and even the *New Yorker*, that proud bastion of the moment-of-truth story that has only recently, and not without controversy, made room in its august confines for the likes of Stephen King.

Over the course of the twentieth century the desire of writers and critics alike to strip away the sticky compound of Orange Crush and Raisinets that encrusts the idea of entertainment, and thus of literature as entertainment, radically reduced our understanding of the kinds of short stories that belong in prestigious magazines or yearly anthologies of the best American short stories. Thanks to the heavy reliance of the new mass media (film, then radio and TV) on adapting and exploiting the more plot-centered literary genres—from *Star Wars* to *Pirates of the Caribbean*, every blockbuster summer film of the past twenty years, almost without exception, fits safely into one or another of the old standby categories—"genre" absorbed the fatal stain of entertainment. Writers—among them some of our finest—kept turning out short stories of post-apocalypse America or Arizona gunmen or hard-boiled detection. But they could no longer hope to see their work published in top-drawer literary magazines, and in the meantime the pulps and the slicks alike dried up, blew away, or stopped publishing short fiction entirely.

And so as with our idea of entertainment, our idea of genre—one of those French words, like *crêpe*, that no one can pronounce both correctly and without sounding pretentious—is of a thing fundamentally, perhaps inherently debased, infantile, commercialized, unworthy of the serious person's attention. The undoubted satisfactions that come from reading science fiction or mystery stories are to be enjoyed only in childhood or youth, or by the adult reader only as "guilty pleasures" (a phrase I loathe). A genre implies a set of conventions—a formula—and conventions imply limitations (the argument goes), and therefore no genre work can ever rise to the masterful heights of true literature, free (it is to be supposed) of all formulas and templates.

This emphasis on the conventionality, the formulaic nature of genre fiction, is at least partly the fault of publishers and booksellers, for whom genre is largely a marketing tool, a package of typefaces and standardized imagery wrapped around a text whose idea of itself as literature, should it harbor one, is more or less irrelevant. "Science fiction," therefore, becomes any book sold in the section of the bookstore so designated. The handsome Vintage Internationals edition of Nabokov's *Ada, or, Ardor*—an extended riff on alternate-world and time theories and a key early example in the retro-futuristic subgenre of science fiction that years later came to be known as steampunk—would look out of place in the science-fiction section, with the blue-foil lettering, the starships, the furry-faced aliens, the electron-starred vistas of cyberspace. *Ada*, therefore, is not science fiction.

Accepting such an analysis sounds like the height of simple-mindedness, yet it is an analysis that you, and I, and both those who claim to love and those who claim to hate science fiction, make, or at least accede to, every time we shop in a bookstore. Though the costly studies and extensive research conducted by the publishing industry remain closely guarded secrets, apparently some kind of awful retailing disaster would result if all the fiction, whether set on Mars or Manhattan, concerning a private eye or an eye doctor, were shelved together, from Asimov and Auster to Zelazny and Zweig. For even the finest writer of horror or sf or detective fiction, the bookstore, to paraphrase the LA funk band War, is a ghetto. From time to time some writer, through a canny shift in subject matter or focus, or through the coming to literary power of his or her lifelong fans, or through sheer, undeniable literary chops, manages to break out. New, subtler covers are placed on these writers' books, with elegant serif typefaces. In the public libraries, the little blue circle with the rocket ship or the magnifying glass is withheld from the spine. This book, the argument goes, has been widely praised by mainstream critics, adopted for discussion by book clubs, chosen by the *Today* show. Hence it cannot be science fiction.

At the same time, of course, there is a difference, right? and sometimes an enormous difference, between, say, Raymond Chandler's "The King in Yellow," and F. Scott Fitzgerald's "Crazy Sunday," even though they are both set in and around Hollywood in roughly the same period. A difference that consists not merely of details of backdrop, diction, mores, costume, weather, etc., nor merely of literary style, nor of the enormously different outlook and concerns of the respective writers. If that was all there was to it, the distinction would be akin to that between *any* two books, chosen at random, from the shelves in the tony part of the bookstore: say, Kathy Acker and William Trevor. (Keep that question in mind, though. Ask yourself just how damned *different* a book has to be, on the inside, from its neighbors, to get it consigned to the genre slums at the local Barnes & Noble. More different than *Moby-Dick* is from *Mrs. Dalloway?*)

No, there are those *conventions* to be considered. These things—mystery, sf, horror—have *rules*. You can go to the How to Write section, away from the teeming ghettos, and find the rules for writing good mystery fiction carefully codified in any number of manuals and guides. Even among experienced, professional writers who have long since internalized or intuited the rules, and thus learned to ignore them, there are, at the very least, particular conventions—the shuttling of the private eye from high society to the lower depths, the function of a literary ghost as punishment for some act of hubris or evil—that are unique to and help to define their respective genres. Many of the finest "genre writers" working today, such as the English writer China Miéville, derive their power and their entertainment value from a fruitful self-consciousness about the conventions of their chosen genre, a heightened awareness of its history, of the cycle of innovation, exhaustion, and replenishment. When it comes to conventions, their central impulse is not to flout or to follow them but, flouting or following, to *play*.

Whether through willfulness, ignorance, or simple amour propre, what tends to be ignored by "serious" writers and critics alike is that the genre known (more imprecisely than any other) as "literary fiction" has rules, conventions, and formulas of its own: the primacy of a unified point of view, for example; letters and their liability to being read or intercepted; the dance of adulterous partners; the buried family secret that curses generations to come; the ordinary heroism of an unsung life. And many of literary fiction's greatest practitioners, from Jane Austen to Angela Carter, Salman Rushdie to Steven Millhauser, display a parallel awareness of the genre's history and conventions, and derive equivalent power and capacity to delight from flouting, mocking, inverting, manhandling, from breaking or ignoring the rules.

Like most people who worry about whether it's better to be wrong or pretentious when pronouncing the word "genre," I'm always on the lookout for a chance to drop the name of Walter Benjamin. I had planned to do so here. I intended to refer to Benjamin's bottomless essay "The Storyteller," and to try to employ the famous distinction he makes in it between the "trading seaman," the storyteller who fetches his miracle tales, legends, and tall stories from abroad, and the "resident tiller of the soil" in whose memory are stored up all the sharp-witted wisdom tales, homely lore, and useful stories of a community. Benjamin implies that the greatest storytellers are those who possess aspects, to some extent, of both characters, and I was thinking that it might be possible to argue that in the world of the contemporary short story the "naturalistic" writers come from the tribe of the community-based lore-retellers, while the writers of fantasy, horror, and sf are the sailors of distant seas, and that our finest and most consistently interesting contemporary writers are those whose work seems to originate from both traditions. But that claim felt a little shaky to me—for one thing, it ignores entirely the work of experimentalists like Ben Marcus or Gary Lutz—and as I invoke the idea of playfulness, of mockery and inversion, the dazzling critic whose work I find myself thinking of most is Lewis Hyde, whose *Trickster Makes This World* rewards rereading every bit as endlessly as any work of Benjamin's.

Hyde's masterpiece concerns the trickster of mythology—
Hermes among the Greeks, the Northmen's Loki, the Native
Americans' Coyote and Raven and Rabbit, the Africans' Eshu
and Legba and Anansi (who reappear in our own folklore in slave
stories of High John de Conquer and Aunt Nancy), Krishna, the
peach-stealing Monkey of the Chinese, and our own friend Satan,
shouting out who killed the Kennedys, when, after all, it was
you and me. Trickster is the stealer of fire, the maker of mischief,
teller of lies, bringer of trouble, upset, and, above all, random
change. And all around the world—think of Robert Johnson
selling his soul—Trickster is always associated with borders, no
man's lands, with crossroads and intersections. Trickster is the
conveyer of souls across ultimate boundaries, the transgressor of
heaven, the reconciler of opposites. He operates through inversion of laws and regulations, presiding over carnivals and feasts of
fools. He is hermaphrodite; he is at once hero and villain, scourge
and benefactor. "He is the spirit of the doorway leading out," as
Hyde writes, "and of the crossroad at the edge of town (the one
where a little market springs up)." For Trickster is also the god
of the marketplace, of the city as intersection of converging roads
and destinies, as transfer point—as the primary locus of entertainment, that powerful means of exchange—and perhaps that is
why cities, Indianapolis excepted, have always been built at the
places where incommensurates meet—sea and land, mountain
and plain, coast and desert. Trickster goes where the action is,
and the action is in the borders between things.

In spite of the continuing disdain or neglect in which most
of the "nonliterary" genres are held, in particular by our finest
writers of short stories, many if not most of the most-interesting
writers of the past seventy-five years or so have, like Trickster,
found themselves drawn, inexorably, to the borderlands. From

Borges to Calvino, drawing heavily on the tropes and conventions of science fiction and mystery, to Anita Brookner and John Fowles with their sprung romance novels, from Millhauser and Thomas Pynchon to Kurt Vonnegut, John Crowley, Robert Aickman, A. S. Byatt, and Cormac McCarthy, writers have plied their trade in the spaces between genres, in the no man's land. These great writers have not written science fiction or fantasy, horror or westerns—you can tell that by the book jackets. But they have drawn immense power from and provided considerable pleasure for readers through play, through the peculiar commingling of mockery and tribute, invocation and analysis, considered rejection and passionate embrace, which are the hallmarks of our Trickster literature in this time of unending crossroads. Some of them have even found themselves straddling that most confounding and mysterious border of all: the one that lies between wild commercial success and unreserved critical acclaim.

It is telling that almost all of the writers cited above, with the notable exception of Borges, have worked primarily as novelists. This is not, I firmly believe, because the short story is somehow inimical to the Trickster spirit of genre-bending and stylistic play. There are all kinds of reasons, some of which have to do with the general commercial decline of the short story and the overwhelming role, which I have only touched on lightly, that business decisions play in the evolution of literary form. But among our most interesting writers of literary short stories today one finds a growing number—Kelly Link, Elizabeth Hand, Aimee Bender, Jonathan Lethem, Benjamin Rosenbaum—working the boundary: "sometimes drawing the line," as Hyde writes of Trickster, "sometimes crossing it, sometimes erasing or moving it, but always there," in the borderlands among regions on the map of fiction. Because Trickster is looking to stir things up, to scramble the conventions, to undo history and received notions of what is art and what is not, to sing for his supper, to find and lose himself in the act of entertaining. Trickster haunts the boundary lines, the margins, the secret shelves between the sections in the bookstore. And that is where, if it wants to renew itself in the way that the novel has done so often in its long history, the short story must, inevitably, go.

MAPS AND LEGENDS

I N 1969, WHEN I was six years old, my parents took out a
Veterans Administration loan and bought a three-bedroom
house in an imaginary city called Columbia. As a pediatri-
cian for the Public Health Service, my Brooklyn-born father was
a veteran, of all things, of the United States Coast Guard (which
had stationed him, no doubt wisely, in the coast-free state of
Arizona). Ours was the first V.A. housing loan to be granted in
Columbia, Maryland, and the event made the front page of the
local paper.

Columbia is now the second-largest city in the state, I am
told, but at the time we moved there, it was home to no more
than a few thousand people—"pioneers," they called themselves.
They were colonists of a dream, immigrants to a new land
that as yet existed mostly on paper. More than four-fifths of
Columbia's projected houses, office buildings, parks, pools,
bike paths, elementary schools, and shopping centers had yet to
be built; and the millennium of racial and economic harmony
that Columbia promised to birth in its theoretical streets and

cul-de-sacs was as far from parturition as ever. In the end, for all its promise and ambition, Columbia may have changed nothing but one little kid. But my parents' decision to move us into the midst of that unfinished, ongoing act of imagination set the course of my life.

In the mid-1960s, a wealthy, stubborn, and pragmatic dreamer named James Rouse had, by stealth and acuity, acquired an enormous chunk of Maryland tobacco country lying along either side of the old Columbia Pike, between Baltimore and Washington. Rouse, often referred to as the inventor of the shopping mall (though there are competing claims to this distinction), was a man with grand ideas about the pernicious nature of the suburb, and about the enduring importance of cities in human life. The City was a discredited idea in those days, burnt and poisoned and abandoned to rot, but James Rouse felt strongly that it could be reimagined, rebuilt, renewed.

He assembled a team of bright men—one of countless such teams of bright men in narrow neckties and short haircuts whose terrible optimism made the sixties such an admirable and disappointing time. These men, rolling up their sleeves, called themselves the Working Group. Like their patron, they were filled with sound and visionary ideas about zoning, green space, accessibility, and the public life of cities, as well as with enlightened notions of race, class, education, architecture, capitalism, and transit. Fate, fortune, and the headstrong inspiration of a theorist with very deep pockets had given them the opportunity to experiment on an enormous scale, and they seized it. Within a relatively short time, they had come up with the Plan.

My earliest memories of Columbia are of the Plan. It was not merely the founding document and chief selling point of the Columbia Experiment. It was also the new town's most treasured possession, the tangible evidence of the goodness of Mr. Rouse's inspiration. The Plan, in both particulars and spirit, was on display for all to see, in a little building (one of Frank Gehry's first built works) called the Exhibit Center, down at the shore of the man-made lake that lay at the heart of both plan and town. This lake—it was called, with the studied, historicist whimsy that contributed so much authentic utopian atmosphere to the town, Lake Kittamaqundi—was tidy and still, rippled by the shining wakes of ducks. Beside it stood a modest high-rise, white and modernistic in good late-sixties *Star Trek* style, called the American City Building. Between this, Columbia's lone "skyscraper," and the Exhibit Center, stretched a landscaped open plaza, lined with benches and shrubbery, immaculate and ornamented by a curious piece of sculpture called the People Tree, a tall dandelion of metal, whose gilded tufts were the stylized figures of human beings. Sculpture, benches, plaza, lake, tower: on a sunny afternoon in 1970 these things had an ideal aspect; they retained the unsullied, infinite perspective of the architect's drawings from which they had so recently sprung.

My parents, my younger brother, and I were shown those drawings, and many more, inside the Exhibit Center. There were projections and charts and explanatory diagrams. And there was a slide show, conducted in one of those long-vanished 1970s rooms furnished only with carpeted cubes and painted the colors of a bag of candy corn. The slide show featured smiling children at play, families strolling along wooded paths, couples working their way in paddleboats across Kittamaqundi or its artificial sister, Wilde Lake. It was a bright, primary-colored world, but the children in it were assiduously black and white. Because that was an integral part of the Columbia idea: that here, in these fields where slaves had once picked tobacco, the noble and extravagant promises that had just been made to black people in the flush of the Civil Rights movement would, at last, be redeemed. That was, I intuited, part of the meaning of the symbol that was reproduced everywhere around us in the Exhibit Center: that we were all branches of the same family; that we shared common roots and aspirations.

Sitting atop a cube, watching the slide show, I was very much taken with the idea—the Idea—of Columbia, but it was as we were leaving the Exhibit Center that my fate was sealed: as we walked out, I was handed a map—a large, foldout map, detailed and colorful, of the Working Group's dream.

The power of maps to fire the imagination is well known. And, as Joseph Conrad's Marlow observed, there is no map so seductive as the one marked, like the flag-colored schoolroom map of Africa that doomed him to his forlorn quest, by doubts and conjectures, by the romantic blank of unexplored territory. The map of Columbia I took home from that first visit was like that. The Plan dictated that the Town be divided into sub-units to be called Villages, each Village in turn divided into Neighborhoods. These Villages had all been laid out and named, and were present on and defined by the map. Many of the Neighborhoods too had been drawn in, along with streets and the network of bicycle paths that knit the town together. But there were large areas of the map that, apart from the Village name, were entirely empty, conjectural—nonexistent, in fact.

The names of Columbia! In the Neighborhood called Phelps Luck, you could find streets with names that were Anglo-whimsical and alliterative: Drystraw Drive, Margrave Mews, Luckpenny Lane; elliptical and puzzling, shorn of their suffixes, Zen: Blue Pool, Red Lake, Spiral Cut; or truly odd: Cloudleap Court, Roll Right Court, Newgrange Garth. It was rumored that the naming of Columbia's one thousand streets had been done by a single harried employee of the Rouse Company who, barred by some kind of arcane agreement from duplicating any of the street names in use in the surrounding counties of Baltimore and Anne Arundel, had turned in desperation from the exhausted lodes of flowers, trees, and U.S. presidents to the works of American writers and poets. (The genius loci of Phelps Luck was Robinson Jeffers.)

I spent hours poring over that map, long before my family ever moved into the house that we eventually bought, with that V.A. loan, at 5179 Eliots Oak Road, in the Neighborhood of Longfellow, in the Village of Harper's Choice. To me the remarkable thing about those names was not their oddity but the simple fact that most of them referred to locations that did not exist. They were like magic spells, each one calibrated to call into being one particular stretch of blacktop, sidewalk, and lawn, and no other. In time—I witnessed it with my own eyes, month by month, year by year—the street demanded by the formula "Darkbush Terrace" or "Night Roost" would churn up out of the Maryland mud and clay, begin to sprout houses, trees, a tidy blue-and-white identifying sign. It was a powerful demonstration to me of the incantatory power of names and naming.

Eventually I tacked the map, considerably tattered and worn, to the wall of my room, on the second floor of our three-bedroom, two-and-a-half-bath pseudocolonial tract house on Eliots Oak Road. In time the original map was joined, there, by a map of Walt Disney World's new Magic Kingdom, and by another of a world of my own devising, a world of horses and tall grass which I called Davoria. I studied the map of Columbia in the morning as I dressed for school (a school without classrooms, in which we were taught, both by racially diverse teachers and by the experience of simply looking around at the other faces in the room, that the battle for integration and civil rights was over, and that the good guys had won). I glanced up at the map at night as I lay in bed, reading *The Hobbit* or *The Book of Three* or a novel set in Oz. And sometimes I would give it a once-over before I set out with my black and white friends for a foray into the hinterlands, to the borders of our town and our imaginations.

Our neighborhood of Longfellow was relatively complete, with fresh-rolled sod lawns and spindly little foal-legged trees, but just beyond its edges my friends and I could ride our bikes clear off the edge of the Known World, into that unexplored blank of bulldozed clay and ribboned stakes where, one day, houses and lives would blossom. We would climb down the lattices of rebar into newly dug basements, dank and clammy and furred with ends of tree roots. We rolled giant spools of telephone cable down earthen mounds, and collected as if they were arrowheads bent nails and spent missile shells of grout. The skeletons of houses, their nervous systems, their subcutaneous layers of insulation, were revealed to us as we watched them growing from the inside out. Later I might come to know the house's eventual occupants, and visit them, and stand in their kitchen thinking, *I saw your house being born.*

In a sense, the ongoing work of my hometown and the business of my childhood coincided perfectly; for as my family subsequently moved to the even newer, rawer Village of Long Reach, and then proceeded to fall very rapidly apart, Columbia and I both struggled to fill in the empty places, to feel our way outward into the mysterious gaps and undiscovered corners of the world. In the course of my years in Columbia, I encountered things not called for by the members of the Working Group, things that were not on the map. There were strange, uncharted territories of race and sex and nagging human unhappiness. And there was the vast, unsuspected cataclysm of my parents' divorce, which redrew so many boundaries, and created, with the proverbial stroke of the pen, vast new areas of confusion and dismay. And then one day I left Columbia and discovered the bitter truth about race relations, and for a while I was inclined to view the lessons I had been taught with a certain amount of rueful anger. I felt that I had been lied to, that the map I had been handed was a forgery. And after all, I would hear it said from time to time, Columbia had failed in its grand experiment. It had become a garden-variety suburb in the Baltimore-Washington Corridor; there was crime there, and racial unrest.

The judgments of Columbia's critics may or may not be accurate, but it seems to me, looking back at the city of my and James Rouse's dreams from thirty years on, that just because you have stopped believing in something you once were promised does not mean that the promise itself was a lie. Childhood, at its best, is a perpetual adventure, in the truest sense of that overtaxed word: a setting-forth into trackless lands that might have come into existence the instant before you first laid eyes on them. How fortunate I was to be handed, at such an early age, a map to steer by, however provisional, a map furthermore ornamented with a complex nomenclature of allusions drawn from the poems, novels, and stories of mysterious men named Faulkner, Hemingway, Frost, Hawthorne, and Fitzgerald! Those names, that adventure, are still with me every time I sit down at the keyboard to sail off, clutching some dubious map or other, into terra incognita.

FAN FICTIONS
ON SHERLOCK HOLMES

1.

ONE HUNDRED AND TWENTY years after his first appearance in print, in the pages of *Beeton's Christmas Annual* for 1887, fans and nonbelievers alike seem to feel compelled to try to explain Sherlock Holmes's lasting appeal, marveling or shaking their heads at it, or both, as if the stories of the adventures with Dr. Watson were a system, like semaphore or the pneumatic post, that ought to have been superseded long since. Such explanations make the case, with varying success, for clever and competent plotting, or the bourgeois thirst for tidy adventure, or nostalgia for a vanished age (Victorian, or adolescent), or the Holmes-Watson dynamic (analyzed perhaps in terms of Jungian or queer theory), or the underlying and still-palpable gentlemanliness of Sir Arthur Conan Doyle, or even, of all things, for the quality of the writing itself, so much higher than it ever needed to be. Inherent in these explanations, buried or explicit, among apologists and critics alike, is a feeling that maybe the fifty-six stories and four short novels that make up the so-called canon (so-called by Sherlockians, about whom more later) are not worthy of such enduring admiration.

Like the flaw in the kabbalists' universe, doubt about the literary merit of the Holmes stories has been present from the first, and the fault lies squarely with the Author. It would be foolish to argue that Conan Doyle despised his Holmes work; it is well known that he regretted it, and disparaged it, saying of Holmes, "I have had such an overdose of [Holmes] that I feel towards him as I do toward *pâté de foie gras*, of which I once ate too much, so that the name of it gives me a sickly feeling to this day." In 1893, in "The Final Problem," a story that reads very much like the act of a desperate man, he made a sincere attempt to have Holmes murdered (by Dr. Moriarty at Reichenbach Falls). But even the first Holmes story, *A Study in Scarlet*, suffers from the author's lack of faith in his creation, since for most of its second part it wanders forlornly, sans Holmes or Watson, amid the Mormon wastes of Utah, where the assassin, later trapped by Holmes, loses the girl he loved.

The next Holmes adventure, *The Sign of Four*, opens with a chapter that features the first of many metacriticisms the detective would offer about the literary efforts of his companion and, by extension, of the cash-strapped young doctor who held their strings: "I glanced over it," Holmes remarks to Watson, referring to *A Study in Scarlet*. He continues,

> Honestly, I cannot congratulate you upon it. Detection is, or ought to be, an exact science, and should be treated in the same cold and unemotional manner. You have attempted to tinge it with romanticism, which produces much the same effect as if you worked

a love-story or an elopement into the fifth proposition of Euclid.

Some of us feel, of course, that the fifth proposition of Euclid would only be improved by a nice juicy elopement. This is a typical bit of good-humored self-mockery, with Conan Doyle displaying the sly wit for which he is too rarely, even by his most ardent admirers, given credit.

While he was busy scorning the Holmes stories and planning Holmes's death, and nursing the suppurating pride of a would-be Walter Scott condemned, first by necessity and then by success, to write popular fiction, Conan Doyle was also, from the beginning, tangibly having fun. It seems to have been characteristic of the man that, as in the above passage, he was usually having it at his own expense.

Like most writers, Conan Doyle wrote for money. His misfortune as an artist was to make piles of it, and become famous around the world, by writing stories he did not consider worthy of his talent, while receiving less credit or pay for works that meant more to him; and to be so freehanded in his philanthropy, wild schemes, and spending habits, and so well endowed with children, that the piles of money were never quite tall enough. Few writers wrote more determinedly for cash than Conan Doyle each time he surrendered his pen to the further elaboration of Sherlock Holmes. That the results of this arrant and effective hackwork have endured so long testifies, in my view, not only to Conan Doyle's art and storytelling gift, and to the magic of the central heroic duo, but to the quickening force, neglected, derided, and denied, of money and the getting of it on a ready imagination.

2.

Secret sharers, deception and disguise, imposture, buried shame and repressed evil, madwomen in the attic, the covert life of London, the concealment of depravity and wonder beneath the dull brick facade of the world—these are familiar motifs of Victorian popular literature. In 1889, J. M. Stoddart, American editor of *Lippincott's Monthly Magazine*, took Oscar Wilde and another writer to lunch, over which he proposed that each man write a long story for his publication. One of his lunch guests that memorable day went off and dreamed up a tale of an uncanny, bohemian, manic-depressive genius who stalks the yellow fog of London, takes cocaine and morphine to ease the torment of living in this "dreary, dismal, unprofitable world," and abates his drug habit by compulsively scheming to peel back the commonplace surface of other people's lives, betraying secret histories of violence and vice. Stoddart published Conan Doyle's second Holmes novel as *The Sign of Four*. Wilde, for his part, turned in *The Picture of Dorian Gray*.

The Victorian habit of seeing double, of reading hidden shame and secret feelings into ordinary human lives, reached its peak with the detective stories of Sigmund Freud, and persists down to our time. It is tempting to read Conan Doyle's biography as a classic Victorian narrative of this kind, of success haunted by shameful failure, marital fidelity that conceals adulterous love, robust scientific positivism that masks deep credulity.

Conan Doyle's life was founded, beginning with his surname, on a series of braided pairs: Irishman and Scotsman, Celt and Englishman, doctor and novelist, anonymous failure and celebrated knight, athlete and aesthete, loving family man and callous wanderer, steadfast husband and hopeless swain, champion of truth and inveterate concealer, advocate of divorce-law reform and anti-suffragist, fife-playing eulogist of Agincourt and heartbroken mourner of the Somme. The series was perfected by an archetypical pair who have only Quixote and Sancho as rivals in the hearts of readers and in the annals of imaginary friendship, that record of wildly limited men who find in each other, and only in each other, the stuff, sense, and passion of one whole man.

Arthur Conan Doyle was the grandson of a caricaturist, the nephew of the designer of the original cover for *Punch*, and the son of Charles Doyle, an architect and painter who died, in a private sanatorium, of drink and of the kind of bitter, self-aware madness that sees itself as damnation through an excess of sanity. His was the kind of madness that reads the random text of the natural world and finds messages and secret connections, the agency of elves and demons and other liminal beings. Charles Doyle burdened his son with a legacy of failure and a treasure as rich and irrelevant as the ritual left by Sir Ralph Musgrave to his baffled heirs: an eccentric way of looking at the world, of making it, against all reason, cohere. The father's fecklessness, epilepsy, alcoholism, and eventual commitment to an institution were for Conan Doyle the black axioms of existence, never acknowledged, sometimes denied.

Conan Doyle's mother, Mary, whom he always called "the Ma'am," seems to have been a model of Victorian motherhood, beribboned and cased in whalebone. She was also a storytelling Irishwoman who thrilled and terrified her children by the fireside on long winter evenings with ghost stories and legends of heroes and the Sidhe. A mother of ten (seven surviving childhood), a model of propriety, modesty, and self-sacrifice, she nonetheless maintained a lifelong relationship with a male lodger fifteen years her junior. Evidence of a sexual liaison between her and the lodger, a pathologist named Bryan Waller, is scanty but suggestive.

Waller's residence in the Doyle house predated the institutional-
ization of Conan Doyle's father, as did the birth of Mary's last child, a
girl who was carefully labeled with the name of Bryan Julia Doyle,
Julia being the name of Waller's mother. It does not require "the
most perfect reasoning and observing mind the world has ever
known" to draw the readiest conclusion. When Waller bought
a house in the Yorkshire countryside, he took Mary and Bryan
Doyle to live with him. He supported young Arthur financially,
and Conan Doyle's fateful decision to attend medical school was
almost certainly determined by the wishes of his mother's mys-
teriously powerful lodger. A reading of Daniel Stashower's biography of Conan Doyle suggests that Bryan Waller was, in practical terms, the most important personage in Conan Doyle's early
life. And yet in all his subsequent published autobiographical
writings and letters he never mentioned him, not once, neither
to thank him nor to settle a score. There is an enigmatic reference
in his memoirs: "My mother had adopted the device of sharing
a large house, which may have eased her in some ways, but was
disastrous in others."

A number of Holmes stories center around the activities of
sinister lodgers in boarding houses, machinating stepparents,
or people who keep their loved ones locked away. Reproachful
ghosts of the immured father, imprisoned for his own supposed
good, can be glimpsed in the eponymous figure of "The Adventure of the Blanched Soldier"—the Boer War veteran hidden in
a "detached building of some size" on the family estate in the
belief that he had contracted leprosy in Africa. It can be seen as
well in the forlorn inhuman visage of the mysterious captive in
"The Yellow Face," and in the ruined figure of "The Crooked
Man," a former soldier who haunts and kills the English officer
who, years ago in India, betrayed him into the hands of torturers.

Detective Freud might well conclude that Conan Doyle never entirely recovered from the pain and humiliation first of watching his mother cuckold his demented father in his own house and then of being obliged to stand by as the old man was packed off to the Montrose Royal Lunatic Asylum, never to return.

The braided pair of Conan Doyle's family history and home life played out in a city that precisely mirrored its duality and duplicity. Even more than London, Edinburgh in the nineteenth century embodied the Jekyll-and-Hyde impulses of the Victorian mind. In London the evil and the good, the public and the private, tended to be presented as near neighbors. They even, as with Henry Jekyll and Edward Hyde, shared the same body. London was figured in jumbles like *The Old Curiosity Shop*, or Krook's shop in *Bleak House*, in landscapes made uniform by fog and mud. Edinburgh, in the time of Conan Doyle's childhood, consisted of two distinct cities, the Old Town and the New. The old medieval center of Edinburgh, "this accursed, stinking, reeky mass of stones and lime and dung," as Thomas Carlyle called it, was notorious throughout Europe for its foulness. Beginning at the end of the eighteenth century it had, like Charles Doyle, been supplanted, though not fully replaced, by a stately city of gray stone, erected on a ridge to the north of the old burgh.

This partly successful act of deliberate moral self-improvement by a city proud of its recent intellectual and commercial accomplishments, and anxious to shed the stigma of its grim parochial past, produced a city with a secret sharer, a striving, rationalistic city whose grid of streets concealed an anxious memory of the bloody old Scots abyss. It also reflected the predicament, and the achievement, of Conan Doyle himself, who lived his dreary and anxious childhood among failure, genteel poverty, and the unimaginable oblivion of his father, on the one hand, and the relative fame and splendor of his successful, artistic Doyle grand-father and uncles in far-off London; between the ever-present specter of ruin and disgrace and the glittering future he dreamed of (and later achieved); between the weird, Irish-Catholic world of his mother's hearth tales and the overtly empirical, Protestant narrative of urban Victorian Scotland.

In medical school at the University of Edinburgh, in the grim Gormenghast heart of the Old Town, Conan Doyle got a decisive demonstration of how his father's way of reading the world for messages could be combined with his mother's gift for making a story. In the fall of 1876, he began attending lectures and work-ing as a clerk in the Royal Infirmary, presided over by Dr. Joseph Bell, FRCS, an ingenious practitioner of what might be called narrative diagnostics. We might also call it prose fiction, or the science of detection.

Joe Bell was a legend at the medical school. His favorite trick—he relished, like the character he would one day inspire, the coup de théâtre—was to diagnose patients in the waiting room of the infirmary without even speaking to them or directly examining them. As Dr. Harold Emery Jones recorded it in a memoir, *The Original of Sherlock Holmes*:

> Gentlemen, a fisherman! You will notice that, though this is a very hot summer's day, the patient is wearing top-boots. When he sat on the chair they were plainly visible. No one but a sailor would wear top-boots at this season of the year... He is concealing a quid of tobacco in the furthest corner of his mouth and manages it very adroitly indeed, gentlemen... Further, to prove the cor-rectness of these deductions, I notice several fish-scales adhering to his clothes and hands, while the odor of fish

announced his arrival in a most marked and striking manner.

The principle behind these feats of inspired guessing, of taking the sum of a set of physical facts, many of them not apparent to the untrained eye, and checking them against an internal reservoir of knowledge based on prior observation—the point of Bell's showmanship—was to awaken the young doctor to the wealth of signs, symptoms, and shortcuts a patient provided. The patient came in spouting and strewing great fiery gouts of information; he or she was a petri dish of facts that it required only patience and a highly trained eye to read and diagnose.

But such observational and interpretational skills were not the whole of the doctoring game, any more than they are for writers or detectives. To succeed as a narrative diagnostician, or a novelist, or a detective, you also needed the art that, if you were Arthur Conan Doyle, you learned from your mother: you needed the feeling for story, both for the "history" to be inferred from the signs and symptoms and for the way that story could be reconstructed, in therapeutic terms, for the benefit of the patient. Bell treated his patients, in part, by telling them their own stories, as if threading a coherent narrative were itself a kind of therapy.

Though Conan Doyle's celebrated failure as a medical practitioner appears to have been exaggerated, it seems clear that he had little luck, and took as little pleasure, in his chosen career. (At least one writer has suggested that Conan Doyle might have managed to kill a patient, through Charles Bovary–like ineptitude or more sinister motives; he did subsequently marry the dead man's sister, and took control of the income that she inherited from her brother.) Like so many Scotsmen of his time, those engineers, overseers, managers, merchant princes, foot soldiers, and rationalizers of the Empire, Conan Doyle had a powerful taste for adventure. In seeking to elude the fate that Waller, his personal Moriarty, had determined for him, Conan Doyle made two inconclusive or ill-fated attempts at becoming a ship's doctor, and a rash and doomed decision to abandon general practice for the study, in Germany, of ophthalmology, in spite of the fact that he barely understood German.

In his late twenties Conan Doyle found himself stuck in a series of difficult, tedious, or failing medical practices, with a young wife whose health was poor and the first of his eventual five children to support, indebted, shut out of the high-end Harley Street clientele, too proud in his agnosticism to go to his devout Doyle relations for help, yearning for the kind of true adventure that his mother's stories had kindled in him. His horizons were lowering, his promise was going unredeemed. He may very well have begun to see himself as lost. He had witnessed Joseph Bell work a kind of salvation, through storytelling, in the infirmary at Edinburgh. It may have been inevitable that his thoughts would turn to Bell now, as, trapped in his desolate consulting rooms, like Holmes taking up the cocaine needle, he took up his pen.

I know I run the risk of hokum in dwelling very long on the connection, at least as old as Rabelais and arguably traceable to the shaman retailing trickster tales by the campfire, between doctors and literature, storytelling and healing. So I'll just mention that when the first dozen Holmes stories were collected and published in *The Adventures of Sherlock Holmes*, a book that made Conan Doyle famous and rich, and saved him forever from the life that he had never resigned himself to living out, they came dedicated to Dr. Joseph Bell.

3.

Though today they are often published without the standard prefix, I think it's important that so many of the fifty-six Sherlock Holmes stories bear the word "Adventure" in their titles: "The Adventure of the Speckled Band," "The Adventure of the Solitary Cyclist." It has become commonplace to view the Holmes tales, and the detective-story tradition that they engendered, as fundamentally conservative. In this reading, the detective, while technically independent of the law, is in truth the dedicated agent of the prevailing social order—a static, hierarchical structure in which murder is an aberration. This was the view Raymond Chandler took of "murder in the Venetian vase," against which he famously posited his "mean streets" theory, in which the autonomous if not anarchist detective operates in a disordered and fluctuating world that can never hope to be restored, in which social position is transient, the law a hopeless fiction, and morality flexible at best.

This view of the Holmes stories as reassuring fables of the fixed values and verities of the Victorian order contains an element of truth. Especially after the first two Holmes novels, *A Study in Scarlet* and *The Sign of Four*, and beginning in 1891 with the first great short story, "A Scandal in Bohemia," Conan Doyle gradually abandoned most of the louche, Wildean touches with which he had initially encumbered the character of Holmes. The outré personal habits, the vampiric hours, the drug use, the willfully outrageous ignorance of "useless facts," such as the order of the solar system or contemporary politics, gave way to a more conventional and cozy sort of eccentricity.

While Holmes is curt with toffs and colonels, he can be a suck-up to royalty, and beneath the surface of the tales glides the majestic shadow of Victoria, emerging only at the end of "The Adventure of the Bruce-Partington Plans," when Holmes, having saved the navy by helping recover the stolen plans for a submarine—"the most jealously guarded of government secrets"—returns from a visit to "a certain gracious lady" wearing an emerald pin in his tie.

Holmes's veneration of methodology, his love of rank and classification (we are informed that Moriarty's henchman, Colonel Sebastian Moran, is "the second most dangerous man in London," and the blackmailer Charles Augustus Milverton is "the worst man in London," and John Clay, who conceived the Red-Headed League, is "the fourth smartest man in London"), his systematic approach to cataloging the minutiae of crime (as in his monograph on the ashes of 140 different varieties of pipe, cigar, and cigarette tobacco) all partake of the Victorian passion for taxonomy, for hierarchies and progressions, for articulating new, rational systems of control. But to read Sherlock Holmes, regardless of his frequent service to Queen and Empire, as a prop and agent of the dominant social order, to regard the function and effect of the stories as characteristic of industrialized, imperialist, Darwinistic, bourgeois, nineteenth-century Britain, the literary kin of Bentham's panopticon or the proposed Cape-to-Cairo railway, misses the point.

In fact, the classic detective story is a device that, with all due respect to Poe and Chevalier Dupin, Conan Doyle invented. This is less a matter of intent, ideology, or effect than of technique. Stories have always manifested a twofold nature, deriving their impact and pleasure in part from the difference between the chronology of the story to be told and the ordering and presentation of that chronology.* Conan Doyle took those two elements—in the form

---

* I am indebted here to Peter Brooks's discussion of "The Musgrove Ritual" in his *Reading for the Plot* (Random House, 1985).

of the crime and the reconstruction of the crime—and completely reengineered them. Like the builder of Skidbladnir, the sailing ship of the Norse gods that could be folded up to fit into your pocket, or an engineer packing an extra million transistors onto a 3 mm chip, Conan Doyle found a way to fold several stories, and the proper means of telling them, over and over into a tightly compacted frame, with a proportionate gain in narrative power. "The Speckled Band" and "The Adventure of the Dancing Men" are storytelling engines, steam-driven, brass-fitted, but among the most efficient narrative apparatuses the world has ever seen. After all these years they still run remarkably well.

The classical Holmes story is framed with Holmes and Watson at home, in their rooms at 221B Baker Street. The frame forms part of a larger, ongoing macro-story of the two companions' lives and long career together, seeing each other through the vicissitudes of, in Watson's case, at least one tragic if vague marriage, and, in the case of Holmes, a cocaine habit, several black depressions, and a self-imposed witness protection program known to Sherlockians as the Great Hiatus, when, after the death of Professor Moriarty, the vengeful henchmen of the Napoleon of Crime made England too hot even for Sherlock Holmes. Set within this frame is the story of a client who has sent up a card or blustered in to see Mr. Holmes, and has now sat down to tell it.

Nearly all the Holmes stories, therefore, are stories of people who tell their stories, and every so often the stories these people tell feature people telling stories (about what they heard or saw, for example, on the night in question), and if this sounds like a dubiously metafictional observation, then we may have forgotten how fundamental such stories-within-stories have always been to popular art from Homer to *Green Acres*, and how lightly worn. The new client tells the story of a recent crime, an apparent crime, or an impending crime, or simply, as in "The Red-Headed League," "The Sussex Vampire," and "The Six Napoleons," recounts a strange and inexplicable incident. As the story proceeds, its teeth engage with the works of the next story, which is the story of the investigation conducted by Holmes and Watson, often with the assistance of one or more slow-witted policemen. The investigation in turn produces the story of how the crime was committed, or of the genuine meaning behind the seemingly inexplicable occurrence. In "The Six Napoleons," for example, what appears to be the story of a rather unlikely anti-Bonapartist serial vandal and murderer bent on smashing busts of Napoleon is found to conceal the story of immigrant Italian artisans trying to recover the "black pearl of the Borgias" that had been hidden in one of the busts.

But that's not all. The solution of the crime is typically not the last of the tellings and retellings that Doyle manages to compact within his endlessly flexible frame: often there remains an account of how the malefactor has been pursued, staked out, hunted down, or how a trap has been laid. Once caught, he or she may introduce an entirely new version of the story, by way of pointing out certain flaws in Holmes's reasoning or confirming his wildest surmises, and then offering reasons for the crime, reasons that can have their roots in yet another story, often one that played out many years before. And then we are back in Baker Street, to be handed over by Watson to the next story.

Writers and storytellers had been nesting their narratives for centuries, of course, in an effort to approximate the networks of story that ramify and complicate our experience of everyday life. But until Conan Doyle, no one had ever hit on a way, or even seen the need, to ensure that the gears of each nested story were fully engaged with those it contained and were in turn contained by. Conan Doyle, in other words, invented a way to tell stories about the construction of stories without the traditional recourse to digression, indirection, or the overtly self-referential. It was a radical step, and it has been paying off for him, and for us, ever since.

But if the Victorian spirit of improvement and efficiency and control—the Cape-to-Cairo spirit—is crucial to the technique of Conan Doyle's stories, what can we say, then, about their function and effect, which the conventional view holds to be to reinforce and to eulogize the iron-and-brick social structure of the Empire?

We can repeat that the stories are, as they insist on being called, adventures. Their function is not to reinforce or validate the dominant social order but to transcend it, abandon it, if only for the space of twenty pages.

A familiar lament of adventure fiction of the late nineteenth and early twentieth century, a lament given its fullest expression in the opening pages of Conan Doyle's novel *The Lost World* (1912) and its most ironic (but no less wistful) in the opening pages of *Heart of Darkness*, is the disappearance of what Conrad's Marlow calls "the blank places on the map." From the time of Odysseus, literary adventurers have sought to write their names in those blank places, and to fetch back stories from them. In this sense, a key part of the business of Empire was to obtain new zones of adventure in which its writers could lay their tales.

Empires are built, however, by laying the groundwork for their own destruction. Subject peoples are educated, organized, given national identities. Any colony made strong enough to survive and flourish becomes too strong to remain a colony. And by the time that Conan Doyle came to write *A Study in Scarlet* in the 1880s, the great explorations undertaken by the Empire, the surveys and royal expeditions of the previous few centuries, had done grave harm to the atlas of adventure. In the years to follow, adventure writers were obliged to devise new strategies. Edgar Rice Burroughs resorted to setting his otherwise classic stories not only in a remote jungle but on Mars or Venus, or in the center of the earth. Robert E. Howard and Talbot Mundy reached back to the pre-exploration past, to prehistory and beyond.

After the technical innovation of packing multiple stories into a tight narrative frame, Conan Doyle's second flash of genius was to find a way to locate the land of adventure within the known world itself, to depict a place beyond laws, where human nature returned to savagery, and where a hero could flourish, right there in the Home Counties. Many of the tales deal with the crimes, misdeeds, and scandals of transported convicts, colonial adventurers, or imperial soldiers returned to England. But these travelers don't merely bring back their tales; they are, as in "The Crooked Man," hunted down by them, haunted by them, killed or forced to kill by the adventures that befell them beyond the sea. As Angus Wilson pointed out in his introduction to *The Return of Sherlock Holmes*, the Holmes stories are replete with imagery of Holmes and Watson as hunters in the jungle, and of men depicted as animals and half-brutes living not on some remote island like Dr. Moreau's, but ten minutes' walk from Marylebone Station. In this moral vacuum Sherlock Holmes is as much a law unto himself as Chandler's Marlowe or Hammett's Continental Op. Repeatedly, persistently, as a matter of existential necessity, in the absence of any real higher authority, he acts to punish those whom the law would exempt, or to allow the guilty to go free. The prevailing view of the Holmes stories as neat little allegories of Victorian positivism is belied by the concluding lines of

"The Cardboard Box," in a passage which tends to be passed over by both those who love the stories and those who dismiss them:

> "What is the meaning of it, Watson?" said Holmes, solemnly, as he laid down the paper. "What object is served by this circle of misery and violence and fear? It must tend to some end, or else our universe is ruled by chance, which is unthinkable. But what end? There is the great standing perennial problem to which human reason is as far from an answer as ever."

Philip Marlowe couldn't have put it better.

4.

A third innovative stroke of Conan Doyle's was to find a new way to play the oldest trick in the book, to revise the original pretense of all adventurers, liars, and storytellers—that every word you are about to hear is true. For at least two hundred years before him, a writer of fiction might employ teasing initials, pseudonyms, and half-censored dates to give the impression that his story had been drawn from some available record, or that the author could personally vouch for its accuracy, but not without harming the innocent, embarrassing the guilty, or defaming the dead. Conan Doyle took this gambit one step further: not only were the Holmes stories presented as factual, with all the necessary names disguised, but their having been published, and subsequently widely read and even enjoyed, was known to their characters. Holmes was not only aware of his status as the subject of Watson's "chronicles," he resented it, and mocked it, even as he profited by the fictional version of the very real success that the stories enjoyed, first in the pages of the *Strand* and *Collier's*, then in the many collected editions.

This kind of heroism, aware of its own literary celebrity, was not entirely new. The heroes of the *Iliad* know that they will one day feature in an epic song. In the second volume of *Don Quixote*, the knight's career is distorted by the first volume's publication (and subsequent piracy). And the opening lines of *The Adventures of Huckleberry Finn* display the same sort of post-publication self-awareness. The difference, and the innovation, is in Dr. Watson. Unlike the singer of the *Iliad*, or the narrator of *Don Quixote*, Watson is at once an active participant in the adventures and their recorder. And unlike Huck Finn, he deliberately presents himself, over and over, as an author preparing accounts for immediate publication, as the man charged with translating Holmes's notes and his own recollections into stories that will, as Holmes sourly puts it, "pander to popular taste." He serves as the guarantor of the stories' "factuality" by experiencing them firsthand, by faithfully transcribing them, and finally by taking the heat for the supposed difficulties and annoyances their publication causes for Holmes. Watson's repeated insistence on his own active part in the stories' finding their way into the hands of the reader—fully half begin with some kind of recognition of their own published status—encourages us to confuse the two doctors, Watson and Conan Doyle, who seem physically and even in their appetites to resemble each other.

Conan Doyle's decision to play this particular fictional trick—to confuse the boundaries between fact and fiction, to write a disguised version of himself into the stories, to have Watson insist on the literal truth of the accounts—had consequences, like all the best tricks, that he did not foresee. On the one hand it produced the thousands of people who have written letters to

Sherlock Holmes over the years and mailed them hopefully to 221B Baker Street (where they are read and answered, to this day, by a specially designated employee of the Abbey National Bank, which has offices at that address). It produced a sense of happy confusion in at least one discerning reader over the years: "Perhaps the greatest of all the Sherlock Holmes mysteries," T. S. Eliot wrote, "is this: that when we talk of him we invariably fall into the fancy of his existence." The pleasure to be derived from pretending to take fiction as fact was also one of the necessary conditions for the rise of the Sherlockians.

The other necessary condition for the rise of that alternately amusing and tedious tribe (not always alternately; to be honest, not always amusing) was the haste and carelessness that so often attended Conan Doyle's writing of the tales. The first twenty-four Holmes stories were written in a period of twenty-nine months, and they are replete with all the contradictions, lacunae, and interesting mistakes of inspiration working under deadline. After the first batch there followed a ten-year interval, corresponding to two years in the world of Holmes and Watson (after the "death" of Holmes, in Moriarty's arms), during which time Conan Doyle forgot a lot of things he had already written about Watson and (the now resurrected) Holmes, producing further contradictions and errors. The perennially thorny question of Watson's wife, Mary, who may or may not have been his first or second wife, and may or may not have died, is the best-known example of this kind of authorial haste.

Conan Doyle, who always wrote quickly and claimed not to revise, seems to have been almost willfully careless when writing his Holmes stories, as if the act of disregarding each story's predecessors and the assertions made therein about Holmes and Watson somehow mitigated their cumulative importance. Or perhaps

Conan Doyle simply could not bear to reread them.

Thus the Holmes stories are constructed around a series of gaps. Some of these gaps are introduced only to be filled by the intuitions and inferences of the Great Detective: they are mysteries to be solved, as when the plans for the Bruce-Partington submarine have disappeared. Then there are the gaps deliberately introduced by Conan Doyle and deliberately left unresolved, in order to lend a greater air of authenticity to his stories. Some of these take the form of those famous allusions to other, unpublished or even unwritten cases that remain, in the view of Watson or Holmes, too scandalous, too libelous, or simply too horrifying to see the light of day. The best known of these is probably that of the Giant Rat of Sumatra, "a story," as we are deliciously warned, "for which the world is not yet prepared."

And then there are all the tantalizing gaps introduced purely through authorial carelessness into the chronology of the stories and the histories of the characters—the lack of information, for example, about Holmes's university career; the strange intermittence and obscure fate of Watson's wife, Mary, who suddenly disappears from the stories, or the oddly migratory wound that Watson received, in his leg or his shoulder, from a Jezail bullet.

Into these gaps has flowed the mock-scholarly tide of the Sherlockians. For the last ninety years, since Monsignor Ronald A. Knox's essay "Studies in the Literature of Sherlock Holmes," a vintage work of deliberate, straight-faced English silliness, writers well known and obscure have been devoting themselves, with a silliness that is sometimes deliberate and faces that are always straight, to trying to settle the questions raised by the gaps that Conan Doyle left lying around the canon. Their labors have produced the vast corpus of Sherlockian essays, papers, and monographs, treating subjects which range from the high incidence in the stories of women named Violet, to the shape and design of the Beryl Coronet. They have sought to analyze the angle at which Colonel Moran must have fired his air gun at the wax dummy of Holmes that Mrs. Hudson so diligently turned around in front of the window of the Baker Street flat, and to settle once and for all the deepest puzzle of all: why Mrs. Watson, or the first Mrs. Watson (in the event that you believe there to have been a second Mrs. Watson), should call her husband James when his name is John. The Sherlockians are playing the game begun by Conan Doyle—the game of pretending that the stories are true, that Holmes and Watson are, or were, real people, that Watson really wrote all the stories and that Conan Doyle was no more than "the Literary Agent." In this sense, the Sherlockians, or Holmesians (rhymes with Cartesians), as they are called in the UK, are all Conan Doyle's fault. He asked for them.

Monsignor Knox's puckish essay was more than a piece of self-parodying scholarship: it was an appropriation, for his own fictive purposes, of the characters, situations, and what would now be termed the "universe" or "continuity" of Conan Doyle's stories. "Studies in the Literature of Sherlock Holmes" led directly, through works like William Baring-Gould's 1962 "biography" of Holmes, *Sherlock Holmes of Baker Street* (essentially a novel in the form of a biography), Billy Wilder's film *The Private Life of Sherlock Holmes* (1970), and Nicholas Meyer's film *The Seven-Per-Cent Solution* (1976), to the contemporary, largely Web-based phenomenon that has devotees of various television programs, cartoons, and film series presenting their own prose versions of the adventures, histories, and sex lives of characters from *Buffy the Vampire Slayer* and *Xena: Warrior Princess*. Such efforts are often derided or dismissed for the amateur productions they are, but the fact is that for at least the past forty years—since (take your pick) the French New Wave, or the Silver Age of Comics, or rock and roll's British Invasion—popular media have been in the hands of people who grew up as passionate, if not insanely passionate, fans of those media: by amateurs, in the original sense of the word.

The first short story that I ever wrote was a tale of Sherlock Holmes, a pastiche written in a clumsy, ten-year-old's version of the narrative voice of Dr. Watson. I was inspired to write my account of Holmes's fateful encounter with Jules Verne's Captain Nemo by having read and adored Nicholas Meyer's then-popular account of the encounter between the detective and Sigmund Freud, which had in its turn been inspired, like every pastiche and Sherlockian monograph before and since, by those magical gaps, those blank places on the map that Conan Doyle left for us, by artlessness and by design.

Readers of Tolkien often recall the strange narrative impulse engendered by those marginal regions named and labeled on the books' endpaper maps, yet never visited or even referred to by the characters in *The Lord of the Rings*. All enduring popular literature has this open-ended quality, and extends this invitation to the reader to continue, on his or her own, with the adventure. Through a combination of trompe l'oeil allusions, of imaginative persistence of vision, it creates a sense of an infinite horizon of play, an endless game board; it spawns, without trying, a thousand sequels, diagrams, and Web sites. In this sense the Sherlockian Game anticipated, and helped to invent, the contemporary fandom that has become indistinguishable from contemporary popular art; it was the Web *avant la lettre*.

And yet there is a degree to which, just as all criticism is in essence Sherlockian, all literature, highbrow or low, from the *Aeneid* onward, is fan fiction. That is why Harold Bloom's notion of the anxiety of influence has always rung so hollow to me. Through parody and pastiche, allusion and homage, retelling and reimagining the stories that were told before us and that we have come of age loving—amateurs—we proceed, seeking out the blank places in the map that our favorite writers, in their greatness and negligence, have left for us, hoping to pass on to our own readers—should we be lucky enough to find any—some of the pleasure that we ourselves have taken in the stuff we love: to get in on the game. All novels are sequels; influence is bliss.

RAGNAROK BOY

I was in the third grade when I first read *D'Aulaires' Book of Norse Myths** and already suffering the changes, the horns, wings, and tusks that grow on your imagination when you thrive on a steady diet of myths and fairy tales. I had read the predecessor, *D'Aulaires' Book of Greek Myths*, and I knew my Old Testament pretty well, from the Creation more or less down to Ruth. There were rape and murder in those other books, revenge, cannibalism, folly, madness, incest, and deceit. And I thought all that was great stuff. Joseph's brothers, enslaving him to some Ishmaelites and then soaking his florid coat in animal blood to horrify their father. Orpheus's head, torn off by a raving pack of women, continuing to sing as it floats down the Hebrus River to the sea: that was great stuff too. Every splendor in those tales had its shadow; every blessing its curse. In those shadows and curses I first encountered the primal darkness of the world, in some of our earliest attempts to explain and understand it.

---

* Then known by its original title, *Norse Gods and Giants*.

I was drawn to that darkness. I was repelled by it, too, but as the stories were presented I knew that I was supposed to be only repelled by the darkness and also, somehow, to blame myself for it. Doom and decay, crime and folly, sin and punishment, the imperative to work and sweat and struggle and suffer the Furies, these had entered the world with humankind: we brought them on ourselves. In the Bible it had all started out with a happy couple in the Garden of Eden; in the Greek myths, after a brief eon of divine patricide and child-devouring and a couple of wars in Heaven, there came a long and peaceful Golden Age. In both cases, we were meant to understand, the world had begun with light and been spoiled. Thousands of years of moralizers, preceptors, dramatists, hypocrites, and scolds had been at work on this material, with their dogma and their hang-ups and their refined sense of tragedy.

The original darkness was still there in the stories, and it was still very dark indeed. But it had been engineered, like a fetid swamp by the Army Corps, rationalized, bricked up, rechanneled, given a dazzling white coat of cement. It had been turned to the advantage of people trying to make a point to recalcitrant listeners. What remained was a darkness that, while you recognized it in your own heart, obliged you all the same to recognize its disadvantage, its impoliteness, its unacceptability, its being wrong, particularly for eight-year-old boys.

In the world of the Northmen, it was a different story.

As the D'Aulaires told it, there was something in Scandinavian mythology that went beyond the straightforward appeal of violence, monstrosity, feats of arms, sibling rivalry, and ripping yarns. Here the darkness was not solely the fault of humans, the inevitable product of their unfitness, their inherent inferiority to a God or gods who—quite cruelly under the circumstances—had created them.

The world of Norse gods and men and giants, which the D'Aulaires depicted in a stunning series of lithographs with such loving and whimsical and brutal delicacy, begins in darkness, and ends in darkness, and is veined like a fire with darkness that forks and branches. It is a world conjured against darkness, in its lee, so to speak; around a fire, in a camp at the edges of a continent-sized forest, under a sky black with snow clouds, with nothing to the north but nothingness and flickering ice. It assumes darkness, and its only conclusion is darkness (apart from a transparently tacked-on post-Christian postlude). Those veins of calamity and violence and ruin that structure it, like the forking of a fire or of the plot of a story, serve to make more vivid the magical glint of goodness that light and color represent. (Everything that is beautiful, in the Norse world, is something that glints: sparks from ringing hammers, stars, gold and gems, the aurora borealis, tooled swords and helmets and armbands, fire, a woman's hair, wine and mead in a golden cup.)

Here the gods themselves are no better or worse, in the moral sense, than humans. They have the glint of courage, of truthfulness, loyalty, wit, and in them maybe it shines a little brighter, as their darkness throws deeper shadows. The morality encoded in these stories is a fundamental one of hospitality and revenge, gift-giving and life-taking, oaths sworn, dooms pronounced, cruel and unforgettable pranks. Moreover (and to my eight-year-old imagination this more than anything endeared them to me), the Norse gods are mortal. Sure, you probably knew that already, but think about it again for a minute or two. *Mortal gods.* Gods whose flaws of character—pride, unfaithfulness, cruelty, deception, seduction—while no worse than those of

Jehovah or the Olympians, will one day, and they know this, prove their undoing.

Start anywhere; start with Odin. First he murders the gigantic, hideous monster who whelped his father, and slaughters him to make the universe. Then he plucks out his own right eyeball and trades it to an ice giant for a sip—a sip!—of water from the well of secret knowledge. Next he hangs himself, from a tree, for nine days and nine nights, and in a trance of divine asphyxia devises the runes. Then he opens a vein in his arm and lets his blood commingle with that of Loki, the worst (and most appealing) creature who ever lived, thus setting in motion the chain of events that will lead to the extinction of himself, everyone he loves, and all the nine worlds (beautifully mapped on the book's endpapers), which he himself once shaped from the skull, lungs, heart, bones, teeth, and blood of his grandfather.

The D'Aulaires capture all of this, reporting it in a straightforward, fustian-free, magical-realist prose that never stops to shake its head or gape at marvels and freaks and disasters, making them seem somehow all the stranger, and more believable. Their spectacular and quirky illustrations (a pair of adjectives appropriate to few illustrators that I can think of offhand) never found a more appropriate subject than the Norse world, with its odd blend of gorgeousness and violence, its wild prodigies and grim humor.

What makes the book such a powerful feat of visual story-telling is the way in which the prose and the pictures (reflecting, perhaps, the marriage and lifelong partnership of the authors, a Norwegian and a Swiss who lived in Connecticut and collaborated on picture books from the 1930s to the late 1960s) complement each other, advance each other's agenda. Almost every page that is not taken up by a giant bursting lithograph of stars and monsters is ornamented with a smaller drawing or with one of the curious, cryptic, twisted little margin-men, those human curlicues of fire, that so disquieted me as a kid and continue, to this day, to freak out and delight my own kids.

Through this intricate gallery of marvels and filigree the text walks with cool assurance, gazing calmly into every abyss, letting the art do the work of bedazzlement while seeing to it that the remarkable facts—the powers and shortcomings of Thor's hammer, Mjolnir, which always returned to its thrower but whose handle was too short to grasp without burning the hand; the strange parentage of Sleipnir, Odin's eight-legged steed, who could carry his rider over land, sea, or air—are laid bare. This simultaneous effect of wonderment and acceptance, this doubled strength, allows the D'Aulaires to balance their re-creation of the Norse world exactly on its point of greatest intensity: the figure of Loki.

Ally and enemy, genius and failure, delightful and despicable, ridiculous and deadly, beautiful and hideous, hilarious and bitter, clever and foolish, Loki is the God of Nothing in Particular yet unmistakably of the ambiguous World Itself. It was in reading this book that I first felt the power of that ambiguity.

When the gods decide to put a wall around Asgard, a giant stone-mason offers to do the onerous work, but demands as payment the hand of the love goddess Freya. This is clearly too steep a price, but Loki persuades the gods to cheat and deceive the mason, promising him Freya if he can complete the work in less than a year. Loki's confidence in his cleverness is typical— no one could fence Asgard in less than a year!—as is his ability to sway others with that confidence, and as is, in the end, the inexorableness with which the stonemason and his gigantic draft horse proceed to build that giant fence of stone. The gods turn in panic and outrage to their glib cousin Loki, with his easy assurances. And then, with days to go and the work nearly done, a beautiful mare appears to distract and seduce the stallion, luring him away from the job site. So the wall goes unfinished, Freya is saved, and the enraged giant pays with his life. But the true ambiguity of Loki is yet to be revealed. The joke, in the end, is always on him: for the giant's stallion succeeds in mounting and siring a foal on Loki, and after several months of embarrassed seclusion the brood-mare god returns to Asgard leading his horse-child behind him. And yet we still have not reached the end of the tale—the typical tale—of Loki's fertile and fatal gift. Because Loki's foal is a wonder horse, the magical Sleipnir, of whom Loki makes a present to his blood-brother Odin: a blessing brought forth out of treachery and lies.

Loki never turned up among the lists of Great Literary Heroes (or Villains) of Childhood, and yet he was my favorite character in the book that was for many years my favorite, a book whose subtitle might have been "How Loki Ruined the World and Made It Worth Talking About." Loki was the god of my own mind as a child, with its competing impulses of vandalism and vision, of imagining things and smashing them. And as he cooked up schemes and foiled them, fathered monsters and stymied them, helped forestall the end of things and hastened it, he was god of the endlessly complicating nature of plot, of storytelling itself.

I grew up in a time of mortal gods who knew, like Odin, that the world of marvels they had created was on the verge, through their own faithlessness and might, of Ragnarok, a time when the best impulses of men and the worst were laid bare in Mississippi and Vietnam, when the suburban Midgard where I grew up was threatened—or so we were told—by frost giants and fire giants sworn to destroy it. And I guess I saw all of that reflected in the D'Aulaires' book. But if those parallels were there, then so was Loki, and not merely in his treachery and his urge to scheme and spoil. Loki was funny—he made the other gods laugh. In his fickleness and his fertile imagination he even brought pleasure to Odin, who with all his well-sipping and auto-asphyxiation knew too much ever to be otherwise amused. This was, in fact, the reason why Odin had taken the great, foredoomed step of making Loki his blood brother—for the pleasure, pure and simple, of his company. Loki was the god of the irresistible gag, the gratuitous punch line, the improvised, half-baked solution—the God of the Eight-Year-Old Boy—and like all great jokers and improvisers, as often the butt and the perpetrator of his greatest stunts.

In the end, it was not the familiar darkness of the universe and of my human heart that bound me forever to this book and the nine worlds it contained. It was the bright thread of silliness, of mockery and self-mockery, of gods forced (repeatedly) to dress as women, and submit to the amorous attentions of stallions, and wrestle old ladies. The D'Aulaires' heterogeneous drawings catch hold precisely of that thread: they are Pre-Raphaelite friezes as cartooned by Popeye's creator, Elzie Segar, at once grandiose and goofy, in a way that reflected both the Norse universe—which begins, after all, with a cow, a great world-sized heifer, patiently, obsessively licking at a salty patch in the primal stew—and my own.

We all grew up—all of us, from the beginning—in a time of violence and invention, absurdity and Armageddon, prey and witness to the worst and the best in humanity, in a world both ruined and made interesting by Loki. I took comfort, as a kid, in knowing that things had always been as awful and as wonderful as they were now, that the world was always on the edge of total destruction, even if, in Maryland in 1969, as today, it seemed a little more true than usual.

ON DAEMONS & DUST

P
ITY THOSE—ADVENTURERS, adolescents, authors of young-adult fiction—who make their way in the borderland between worlds. It is at worst an invisible and at best an inhospitable place. Build your literary house on the border-lands, as the English writer Philip Pullman has done, and you may find that your work is recommended by booksellers, as a stopgap between installments of *Harry Potter*, to children who cannot (one hopes) fully appreciate it, and to adults, disdainful or baffled, who "don't read fantasy." Yet all mystery resides there, in the margins, between life and death, childhood and adulthood, Newtonian and quantum, "serious" and "genre" literature. And it is from the confrontation with mystery that the truest stories have always drawn their power.

Like a house on the borderlands, epic fantasy is haunted: by a sense of lost purity and grandeur, deep wisdom that has been forgotten, Arcadia spoilt, the debased or diminished stature of modern human-kind; by a sense that the world, to borrow a term from John Clute, the Canadian-born British critic of fantasy and science fiction, has "thinned." This sense of thinning—of there having passed a Golden Age, a Dreamtime, when animals spoke, magic worked, children honored their parents, and fish leapt filleted into the skillet—has haunted the telling of stories from the beginning. The words "once upon a time" are in part a kind of magic formula for invoking the ache of this primordial nostalgia.

But serious literature, so called, regularly traffics in the same wistful stuff. One encounters the unassuageable ache of the imagined past, for example, at a more or less implicit level, in American writers from Cooper and Hawthorne through Faulkner and Chandler, right down to Steven Millhauser and Jonathan Franzen. Epic fantasy distills and abstracts the idea of thinning— maps it, so to speak; but at its best the genre is no less serious or literary than any other. Yet epic fantasies, whether explicitly written for children or not, tend to get sequestered in their own section of the bookstore or library, clearly labeled to protect the unsuspecting reader of naturalistic fiction from making an awkward mistake. Thus do we consign to the borderlands our most audacious retellings of what is arguably one of the two or three primal human stories: the narrative of Innocence, Experience, and, straddling the margin between them, the Fall.

Any list of the great British works of epic fantasy must begin with *Paradise Lost*, with its dark lord, cursed tree, invented cosmology, and ringing battle scenes, its armored, angelic cavalries shattered by demonic engines of war. But most typical works of contemporary epic fantasy have (consciously at least) followed Tolkien's model rather than Milton's, dressing in Norse armor and Celtic shadow the ache of Innocence Lost, and then, crucially, figuring it as a landscape, a broken fairyland where brazen experience has replaced the golden days of innocence; where, as in *The Chronicles of Narnia*, it is "always winter and never Christmas."

A recent exception to the Tolkienesque trend is Pullman's series of three novels, *The Golden Compass*, *The Subtle Knife*, and *The Amber Spyglass* (with a promised fourth, *The Book of Dust*), which reshuffle, reinterpret, and draw from Milton's epic both a portion of their strength and their collective title: *His Dark Materials*.

There are broken lands in *His Dark Materials*—there are entire broken universes, in fact, whose vital stuff is leaking from them into the Miltonic abyss at a frightening rate. But the central figuring of Innocence and the Fall Pullman accomplishes neither through the traditional mapping of a landscape nor, as in Jack Vance's classic *The Dying Earth*, through melancholy reiteration of the depleted catalog of a once-vast library of magical texts and spells. Instead, Pullman has looked around at this broken universe of ours, in its naturalistic tatters, and has indicated, like Satan pointing to the place on which Pandemonium will rise, the site of our truest contemporary narratives of the Fall: in the lives, in the bodies and souls, of our children.

2.

Lyra Belacqua is a girl of ten or eleven when *The Golden Compass*, the first volume of the series, begins. Her parentage, in the traditional manner, is uncertain, at least to her. She is headstrong, cheerful, forthright, loyal, and articulate, rather in the Dorothy Gale style of female fantasy heroines. She is also an uncouth, intractable, manipulative liar, and occasionally stupid. The first time we encounter her, she is engaged in an act of inadvisable disobedience—trespassing in the Retiring Room at

Jordan College, Oxford, which is strictly off-limits to all but Scholars—one whose consequences, which she imagines as no worse than chastisement, will include but not be limited to wide-scale ecological disaster and the death of her best friend. She has, in other words, a complexity of character, and a tragic weakness unusual for a work of children's literature, and in fact the question of whether or not *His Dark Materials* is meant or even suitable for young readers not only remains open but grows ever more difficult to answer as the series progresses. This indeterminacy of readership—the way Pullman's story pulses fitfully between the poles of adult and children's fiction, illuminating by weird flashes that vague middle zone known in the librarian trade as YA—is, as I have already suggested, itself a figuring- or working-out of the fundamental plot of *His Dark Materials*, which turns, and turns again, on the question of what becomes of us, of our bodies and our souls, as we enter the borderland of adolescence.

Lyra lives in a room at Jordan College, where she has led a half-feral, largely pleasurable life as the seditious, indifferently educated ward of the college, looked after by a gruff old housekeeper and a faculty of male scholars who have no idea what to make of or do with her. Her childhood, an unbroken series of small adventures, hair-raising exploits, and minor wars among the local tribes of Oxford's children, is evoked by Pullman in the first book's opening chapters with verve, humor, and the special poignance of his foreknowledge, and our strong suspicion, that it is Lyra's childhood—and indeed Childhood itself—that will prove to be the irrecoverable paradise, the Dreamtime, of his story.

There is, of course, no Jordan among the colleges of Oxford University. Lyra's Oxford exists in a different universe, one in which, as in our own, it is a primary center of learning and scholarship for England, Europe, and the world, has deep ecclesiastical roots, and sits astride the Thames River, on a bend known locally as the Isis. But in Lyra's world, though it strongly resembles our own in many ways—including possessing what appears to be an identical geography—evolution and history have taken different bends. Here, during the Reformation, the Holy See was transferred from Rome to Geneva; at some point John Calvin became pope. Somehow this, and a number of other premises, most of which Pullman leaves unstated, form a syllogism whose conclusion is a world united under the rule of a powerfully repressive Church Triumphant that is itself fatally divided among warring factions of bishops and prelates banded into orders whose names are at once bland, grand, and horrible: the Consistorial Court of Discipline, the General Oblation Board (charged with preparing oblations, or offerings, whose nature is at first a source of considerable mystery). What we know as science, in particular physics, is viewed in Lyra's world as a subject fit for philosophers and above all for theologians—the study of fundamental particles is known there as experimental theology. Its discoveries are subject to ultimate review by the Church, and painful is the reward awaiting those, like a certain Russian Dr. Rusakov, who posit the existence of phenomena that violate Church teaching.

Lyra's world, with its shuffled deck of underlying premises, is technologically accomplished in ways that equal and even exceed our own—helped in this regard by its willingness to view as controllable natural phenomena what our world would call magic—and in other ways strangely retarded or perverse. Electric power is widely in use, though it is known as "anbaric power" (the terms are etymologically akin, deriving from the Greek and Arabic words for amber), produced by great river-spanning dynamos and "atom-craft" plants, but guns have no ascendancy, refrigeration and the science of food preservation appear to be unknown, and computers and automobiles are little in evidence. Instead travel proceeds on foot, by boat, or by that colophon of alternate-world fiction from *Ada* to *The League of Extraordinary Gentlemen*, the grand zeppelin liner. But for all its neo-Edwardian style, Lyra's Oxfordshire appears largely to remain sunk in the Middle Ages—agrarian, semifeudal, reckoning its calendar by harvest and fair and by the seasonal comings and goings of a small, fierce nation of people known as Gyptians, led by their king, John Faa, whose name appears, in our world, in a well-known fifteenth-century English ballad about a gypsy king.

While Pullman alludes to Nabokov (one of the characters in *The Subtle Knife* voyages to Nova Zembla), his paired Oxfords stand in a very different relation from that of *Ada*'s Terra and Antiterra, which reflect and comment only upon each other, locked in a transdimensional self-regard which in turn mirrors that of the vain Van Veen. Instead, Pullman has consciously and overtly founded the structure of his fictional universe on the widely if not universally accepted "many-worlds hypothesis," derived from quantum physics—in *His Dark Materials* there will eventually turn out to be (rather conservatively) "millions" of such worlds, though in the end Pullman has only guided us through half a dozen of them.* Lyra's and ours are only two among the infinite number of possible Oxfords, all of which, according to the hypothesis at its most extreme, exist.

---

* Pullman avoids use of the term "multiverse," arguably coined by the greatest writer of post-Tolkien British fantasy, Michael Moorcock, to whose work Pullman's is clearly indebted.

Pullman's use of such avant-garde scientific notions as the multiverse and dark matter (more on that later) might incline one to slap the label of "science fiction" onto his work along with "epic fantasy," "YA," and "alternate-world fiction"; but the quantum physics in *His Dark Materials* is mostly employed as a rationale for the standard world-hopping that heroes and heroines of fantasy have been engaging in from Gilgamesh onward. More interesting is Pullman's understanding of the metaphoric power of the many-worlds theory. An endlessly ramifying series of possibility-worlds, diverging and diverging again with each alteration in state, each tiny choice made, each selection of B over A: this may or may not be physics, but it is indisputably storytelling. And Pullman, as it turns out, is an unabashed concocter of stories, with a deep, pulpy fondness for plot. He is also, in the great tradition of unabashed concocters of stories, a highly self-conscious storyteller. By the end of *The Amber Spyglass*, one has come to see Pullman's world-calving imagination, to see Imagination itself, as the ordering principle, if not of the universe itself, then of our ability to comprehend, to wander, and above all to love it.

3.

However far the narrative may wander, the action of *His Dark Materials* centers tightly, even obsessively, on the interrelation of two of Pullman's many felicitous inventions: daemons and Dust.

The goddess of writers was smiling upon Philip Pullman on the day he came up with the idea for daemons. These are, in Lyra's world, the inseparable life companions of every human being. Daemons take the shapes of animals, but they have reason and the power of speech. Lyra's is named Pantalaimon—she calls him Pan—and at first we take him to be her animal familiar, but we soon learn that he is in fact the equivalent of what is known in our world as the soul. The bond between human and daemon is fundamental, essential, empathic, and at times telepathic. When a daemon's human being dies, its own life ends; the daemon winks out of existence, snuffed out like a candle flame. Pan, like all children's daemons, has not yet "settled"—that is, he can take on, at will, the shape of any animal he wishes, a power he will retain until Lyra reaches puberty. When Pan is frightened or anxious to conceal himself, he is a moth, or a mouse; when he wishes to intimidate or to repel attack, he becomes a snarling wildcat; when Lyra is feeling lonely or cold, he becomes a soft, warm ermine and drapes himself tenderly around her neck.

As the story unfolds, new wrinkles and refinements in the relationship between human and daemon keep occurring to Pullman, and he reports them to us at once with the palpable storyteller's excitement that animates (and at times undermines) the entire series: while people generally have daemons of the opposite gender to their own, some rare oddballs have a same-sex daemon; people tend to get the daemons they deserve (schemers have snake daemons, servants have dog daemons); there is a painful limit to the distance by which a human and a daemon can stand to be separated, except in the case of the witches of the North—those Lapland witches mentioned by Milton in Book II of *Paradise Lost?*—who undergo a fearsome initiation rite that enables them and their daemons to travel separately. And so on. My then-eight-year-old daughter expressed what I imagine is a near-universal response of readers, young and old, to *His Dark Materials* (and probably the ultimate secret of the series' success): "I wonder what kind of daemon I would have!"

When we meet them, Lyra and her daemon are spying on hastily organized preparations for the return to Jordan College

74

of the man she believes to be her uncle, Lord Asriel, an explorer and inventor of formidable reputation. Pan has advised against this foray into the forbidden Retiring Room, and he flutters anxiously on her shoulder, having taken for the moment the fearful, flighty form of a moth. It is here, hidden in a wardrobe full of scholars' gowns, that Lyra and we first encounter the sparkling puzzle of Dust.

Lord Asriel has just returned from the North, where he led an expedition (lovingly outfitted by Pullman, like all the novels' several expeditions, with the full Shackletonian panoply of late-Victorian explorers' gear) to observe the phenomena known, after the Church-burned heretic who first described them, as Rusakov particles, or Dust. All of the novels' villains, demagogues, and amoral researchers, as well as a number of its finer, nobler characters—Pullman, true to his YA roots, has a tendency to lay on the fine and the noble with a rather heavy spackling knife—believe, or come to believe, that the continued existence of the theocratic, Church-determined, hierarchical universe as they know it depends on understanding the mysterious charged particles known in our world as dark matter and in Lyra's as Dust. These invisible particles seem to be connected in some way to the aurora borealis,[†] and they have the curious property (as Lord Asriel proceeds to demonstrate by means of a photographic process of his own invention, with Lyra and Pan, concealed in the wardrobe, hanging on his every word) of being powerfully attracted to adult human beings, settling on them like dander or snow, while appearing to be completely uninterested, if particles can be said to take interest (and they can!), in children.

[†] The original British title of *The Golden Compass* is *Northern Lights*.

Lord Asriel has returned from the North to hit up the College for more funding, ostensibly so that he can continue his purely scientific research into the puzzling nature of Dust. In reality he intends to follow the trail of falling Dust out of Lyra and her daemon's world and into another. He doesn't mention this, however, or that implementing his plan of opening a breach through the boreal "thin patch" will require the sacrifice of a child by means of a horrific brand of metaphysical vivisection known as "intercision."

Intercision is also the business of the General Oblation Board, an arm of the Church that has recently begun a spectacular rise to power under the direction of Mrs. Coulter, its lay chairman. Mrs. Coulter is, until she receives an unfortunate first name (the far too *British Vogue* "Marisa") and, even more unfortunately, a heart, somewhere around the second quarter of *The Amber Spyglass*, one of the great villains of recent popular literature, right up there, in viciousness, strength, intelligence, and inexorableness, with *Lonesome Dove*'s (unredeemed to the end) Blue Duck. Mrs. Coulter, beautiful, elegant, capable of simulating terrible charm and warmth, her natural mode a fittingly polar coldness, accompanied everywhere by her truly scary golden monkey daemon, has the power, like all good femmes fatales, to cloud men's minds.

Under her spell, and frightened by the implications of Dust's evident attraction to experience in the Blakean sense, to Fallenness—believing that Dust may be the physical manifestation of Original Sin itself—the Church leadership has authorized Mrs. Coulter to lead a northern expedition of her own, one that will seek to determine whether Dust—Sin—can be forestalled, fended off, or eliminated entirely, by the intercision of a child before his or her daemon has "settled." Naturally this course of research, carried out at a remote post in the Arctic, where Dust streams most plentifully, requires a steady supply of preadolescent subjects. Under Mrs. Coulter's orders, teams of child-snatchers—known semimythically among the local children as "Gobblers"—fan out across England, baiting their traps with sweets and kindness. When her best friend at the College, a servant's child named Roger, is stolen away by Mrs. Coulter's General Oblation Board, Lyra determines to set off for the North and save him.

The first volume of the sequence, *The Golden Compass*, is taken up with the competing schemes of Lord Asriel and Mrs. Coulter to understand and if possible control Dust, and with Lyra's quest to find Roger and at the same time to convey to Lord Asriel (funded again and back in the North) a marvelous contraption called an alethiometer. The alethiometer is Pullman's third great invention, after daemons and Dust. A beautiful instrument of gold and crystal, engraved with an alphabet or tarot of conventional symbols and fitted with knurls and indicator needles, the alethiometer will answer any question put to it, though it will not predict the future. When it comes to reading the alethiometer, a skill that normally demands a lifetime of training and study, Lyra proves to be a natural.

Under the alethiometer's tutelage, and with the help of a troop of stout Gyptians, Lyra makes her way north, learning, in the usual way of such journeys, even more about herself and her history than about the world she lives in, and discovering that there is a prophecy among the witches that she seems to be about to fulfill. Along the way she encounters an adventurer named Lee Scoresby, a Texan from New Denmark (her world's U.S.), who comes equipped with a hot-air balloon and a greasepaint-Texan manner that will be familiar to readers of Buchan and Conan Doyle; and the appealing Iorek Byrnison, who in spite of his Nordic name is a polar bear, or a kind of polar bear, polar bears in Lyra's world having evolved opposable thumbs (they are mighty smiths) and the power of speech. Interestingly it is Byrnison the bear and not Scoresby the Texan who plays the Lee Marvin role in this novel, rousing himself from an alcoholic miasma of failure—it all turns on a question of bear politics— through admiration of the gifted and fiery girl.

With the help of her companions, and following a number of hectic battles and one chilling scene of paternal anagnorisis (moment of recognition), Lyra fulfills her pledge to deliver the alethiometer to Lord Asriel and rescue Roger and the other stolen children—though with results that she finds, in the former instance, disappointing (Lord Asriel is stricken with a weird horror when he recognizes Lyra at the door of his polar fortress of solitude) and, in the latter, unexpectedly tragic, as poor Roger provides the means for Lord Asriel's breaching of the border between worlds.

The second volume, *The Subtle Knife*, introduces a new character, one who will come to assume an equal stature in the series to Lyra's. He is Will Parry, a boy of roughly Lyra's age who lives in a drab suburb near Oxford—our Oxford, this time. When we meet him, Will is struggling to protect himself and his mother—his father, an explorer and former Royal Marine, disappeared years before—from some sinister men, vaguely governmental, who are after the letters that Mr. Parry sent back home from the Arctic just before his disappearance. It's a struggle for Will because his mother is no help at all; she's mad, affected by some kind of obsessive-compulsive disorder that leaves her barely functional as a human being, let alone as a mother. For years, young Will has been handling all the duties and chores that his mother can't manage, and caring for her on her bad days, working very hard to maintain the illusion that all is well in the Parry house. He doesn't want them to come and take his mother away from him.

When the government agents grow overbold and confront his mother directly, Will realizes that his life is about to change. There is a poignant scene in which, seeking out the only kind, trustworthy person he has ever known—he has no friends—he leaves his bewildered mother with a nearly equally bewildered older woman who was once, briefly, his piano teacher, Mrs. Cooper (the name alludes to Susan Cooper, author of the beloved *The Dark Is Rising* sequence of novels, whose central protagonist is a boy named Will). Then he finds and collects his father's letters, accidentally killing one of the government men in the process, and flees.

He flees—though this is not, of course, his intention at first—into another world, to a place called Cittàgazze, the City of the Magpies. For it turns out that there are other ways to pass among the worlds than by Lord Asriel's costly method of child-sacrifice and transdimensional demolition. One can, if properly equipped, simply cut a hole in the membrane that separates realities from each other. To do this one needs a knife—a very special kind of knife, naturally: a subtle knife. There is only one of these in all the worlds; it was forged, some three hundred years ago, by the savants of the Torre degli Angeli, a kind of scientific academy housed in a castellated tower in Cittàgazze. They forged it; and then, unfortunately, they began to use it, cutting their way from world to world, leaving a trail of carelessly abandoned holes such as the one through which Will, fleeing the murder he has committed, tumbles.

In the desolate, De Chirico streets of Cittàgazze, Will Parry meets Lyra; she has come from her world through the breach

Lord Asriel created, hoping to solve the riddle of Dust, intuiting that contrary to the teachings of the Church, it may in fact be a blessing and not a curse. Lyra is at first as startled to see a living, thriving boy with no daemon as Will is to watch her pet cat transform itself into a stoat. But the two children, alone in a world of wild menacing orphans (all the adults here having fled or been devoured), form a bond and make common cause: Will, following hints in John Parry's letters, intends to track his father down. And Lyra, taking instruction from the alethiometer, determines to help him. In an exciting scene Will inherits the subtle knife, and away the two children go, in search of John Parry and the riddle of Dust.

They are far from alone in these pursuits; a host of adult characters—Lee Scoresby, Iorek Byrnison, Mrs. Coulter, Lord Asriel, the witch Serafina Pekkala, a nun turned theoretical physicist of our world named Mary Malone—follow courses that parallel, intersect, or shadow Will and Lyra's. *The Golden Compass* is Lyra's book, structured around her and presented almost wholly through her point of view, and as such it reads very much like a traditional quest story. *The Subtle Knife*, with its shifting points of view and its frequent presentation of adult perspectives on Lyra and Will, has much more the flavor of a thriller. It is unflaggingly inventive, chilling, and persuasive, has a number of gripping action sequences, and ends with a thrilling zeppelin battle in the Himalayas. But something—the pleasure inherent, perhaps, in the narrative unfolding of a single consciousness—is lost in the transition from first volume to second; and though Pullman's storytelling gifts reach their peak in *The Subtle Knife*, the sequence itself never quite recovers from this loss.

Nevertheless, the proliferation of points of view and different quests, which expands still further in the third volume, *The*

Amber Spyglass, is itself a kind of figure for the necessary loss of innocence, for the *felix culpa*, or Fortunate Fall, that lies at the heart of this deliberate, at times overdeliberate rejoinder or companion to *Paradise Lost*. As Lyra's daemon comes ever closer to settling in its final form, the narrative itself grows ever more unsettled; for a single point of view is a child's point of view, but a multiple point of view is the world's. And the settling of a daemon into a single form with the onset of adulthood, Pullman tells us, represents not simply a loss of the power to change, of flexibility and fire; it also represents a gain in the power to focus, to concentrate, to understand, and, finally, to accept: a gain in wisdom. Even Mrs. Coulter, that wicked, wicked woman, is granted her place in the narrative, and Pullman (not entirely successfully) makes us privy to her heart.

I have resisted trying to summarize, and thereby spoil, the vast, complicated plot of *His Dark Materials*, which runs to more than twelve hundred pages. But there is no way to form or convey a judgment of the sequence without giving away the name, alas, of the ultimate, underlying villain of the story, a character whose original scheme to enslave, control, and dominate all sentient life in the universe is threatened first by the implications of Dust as *felix culpa* and then by the ambition of the new Lucifer, Lord Asriel, with whose Second Rebellion the plot of *The Amber Spyglass* is largely concerned. The gentleman's name is Jehovah.

4.

The Amber Spyglass was awarded the *Guardian*'s fiction prize for 2000, the first time that a novel ostensibly written for children had been so honored. Shortly afterward, the new laureate stirred up controversy by publicly attacking his fellow Oxonian C. S.

Lewis, and in particular the *Narnia* books (which also begin, of course, in a wardrobe), calling them racist, misogynist, and allied with a repressive, patriarchal, idealist program designed to quash and devalue human beings and the world—the only world—in which we have no choice but to live and die.

Or something like that. I confess to taking as little interest in the question of organized Christianity's demerits as in that of its undoubted good points, in particular when such a debate gets into the works of a perfectly decent story and starts gumming things up. My heart sank as it began to dawn on me, around the time that the first angels begin to show up in *The Subtle Knife*, that there was some devil in Pullman, pitchfork-prodding him into adjusting his story to suit both the shape of his anti-Church argument (with which I largely sympathize) and the mounting sense of self-importance evident in the swollen (yet withal sketchy) bulk of the third volume and in the decreasing roundedness of its characters. By the end of the third volume, Lyra has lost nearly all the tragic, savage grace that makes her so engaging in *The Golden Compass*; she has succumbed to the fate of Paul Atreides, the bildungsroman hero turned messiah of *Dune*, existing only, finally, to fulfill the prophecy about her. She has harrowed Hell (a gloomy prison yard, according to Pullman, less Milton than Virgil, home of whispering ghosts cringing under the taunts and talons of the screws, a flock of unconvincing harpies), losing and then regaining her daemon-soul; she has become, like all prophesied ones and messiahs, at once more and less than human.

This is a problem for Pullman, since *His Dark Materials* is explicitly—and materially, and often smashingly—about humanity. That's the trouble with Plot, and its gloomy consigliere, Theme. They are, in many ways, the enemies of

Character, of "roundedness," insofar as our humanity and its convincing representation are constituted through contradiction, inconsistency, plurality of desire, absence of abstractable message or moral. It's telling that the epithet most frequently applied to God by the characters in *His Dark Materials* is "the Authority." This fits in well with Pullman's explicit juxtaposition of control and freedom, repression and rebellion, and with his championing of Sin, insofar as Sin equals Knowledge, over Obedience, insofar as that means the kind of incurious acceptance urged on Adam by Milton's Raphael. But the epithet also suggests, inevitably, the Author, and by the end of *His Dark Materials* one can't help feeling that Will and Lyra, Pullman's own Adam and Eve—appealing, vibrant, chaotic, disobedient, murderous—have been sacrificed to fulfill the hidden purposes of their creator. Plot is fate, and fate is always, by definition, inhuman.

Thank God, then, for the serpent, for the sheer, unstoppable storytelling drive that is independent of plot outlines and thematic schemes, the hidden story that comes snaking in through any ready crack when the Authority's attention is turned elsewhere. In *Paradise Lost*, we find ourselves, with Blake, rooting for the poets, for the "devil's party." Satan is one of us; so much more so than Adam or Eve. There's a puzzling pair of exchanges in *The Amber Spyglass*, when Lyra attempts to cheer the denizens at the outskirts of Hell, and sing for her supper, by telling them the story of her and Will's adventures up to that point. Like the accounts that Odysseus gives of himself, Lyra's is a near-total fabrication, replete with dukes and duchesses, lost fortunes, hairbreadth escapes, shipwrecks, and children suckled by wolves, and it's meant to be absurd, "nonsense"; but in fact it's made out of precisely the same materials, those dark materials of lies and adventure, as *His Dark Materials*. And the poor dwellers of the suburbs of the dead, listening to Lyra's tale, are comforted. It comes as a surprise, then, when having reached the land of the dead itself, Lyra's tale, with the apparent complicity of the narrator, is violently rejected by the Harpy, that humorless, bitter, inhuman stooge of God: "Liar!" Later, the Harpy hears Lyra's more accurate account of her voyage and approves it, because, apparently, it sticks to the facts and includes references to the substance of the corporeal world that the Harpy has never known. But so does the lie; and so, in spite of, or in addition to, its stated, anti-Narnian intentions, does *His Dark Materials*.

Lies, as Philip Pullman knows perfectly well, tell the truth; but the truth they tell may not be that, or not only that, which the liar intends. The secret story he has told is not one about the eternal battle between the forces of idealist fundamentalism and materialist humanism. It is a story about the ways in which adults betray children; how children are forced to pay the price of adult neglect, cynicism, ambition, and greed; how they are subjected to the programs of adults, to the General Oblation Board. Each of its child protagonists has been abandoned, in different ways, by both of his parents, and while they find no shortage of willing foster parents, ultimately they are betrayed and abandoned by their own bodies, forced into the adult world of compromise and self-discipline and self-sacrifice, or "oblation," in a way that Pullman wants us—and may we have the grace—to understand as not only inevitable but, on balance, a good thing.

Still, we can't help experiencing it—as we experience the end of so many wonderful, messy novels—as a thinning, a loss not so much of innocence as of wildness. In its depiction of Lyra's breathtaking liberty to roam the streets, fields, and catacombs of Oxford, free from adult supervision, and of Will's Harriet the Spy–like ability to pass, unnoticed and seeing everything, through the worlds of adults, a freedom and a facility that were once, but are no longer, within the reach of ordinary children; in simply taking the classic form of a novel that tells the story of children who adventure, on their own, far beyond the help or hindrance of grown-ups, *His Dark Materials* ends not as a riposte to Lewis or a crushing indictment of authoritarian dogma but as an invocation of the glory, and a lamentation for the loss, which I fear is irrevocable, of the idea of childhood as an adventure, a strange zone of liberty, walled, perhaps, but with plenty of holes for snakes to get in.

KIDS' STUFF

OR AT LEAST THE first forty years of their existence, from
the Paleozoic pre-Superman era of *Famous Funnies* (1933)
and *More Fun Comics* (1936), comic books were widely
viewed, even by those who adored them, as juvenile: the ultimate
greasy kids' stuff. Comics were the literary equivalent of bubble-
gum cards, to be poked into the spokes of a young mind, where
they would produce a satisfying—but entirely bogus—rumble
of pleasure. But almost from the first, fitfully in the early days,
intermittently through the fifties, and then starting in the mid-
sixties with increasing vigor and determination, a battle has been
waged by writers, artists, editors, and publishers to elevate the
medium, to expand the scope of its subject matter and the range
of its artistic styles, to sharpen and increase the sophistication of
its language and visual grammar, to probe and explode the limits
of the sequential panel, to give free reign to irony, tragedy, autobiography, and other grown-up-type modes of expression.

Also from the first, a key element—at times the central element—of this battle has been the effort to alter not just the

medium itself but the public perception of the medium. From the late, great Will Eisner's lonely insistence, in an interview with the *Baltimore Sun* back in 1940 (*1940!*), on the artistic credibility of comics, to the nuanced and scholarly work of recent comics theorists, both practitioners and critics have been arguing passionately on behalf of comics' potential to please—in all the aesthetic richness of that term—the most sophisticated of readers.

The most sophisticated, that is, of *adult* readers. For the adult reader of comic books has always been the holy grail, the promised land, the imagined lover who will greet the long-suffering comic-book maker, at the end of the journey, with open arms, with acceptance, with approval.

A quest is often, among other things, an extended bout of inspired madness. Over the years this quest to break the chains of childish readership has resulted, like most bouts of inspired madness, in both folly and stunning innovation. Into the latter category we can put the work of Bernard Krigstein or Frank Miller, say, with their attempts to approximate, through radical attack on the conventions of panel layouts, the fragmentation of human consciousness by urban life; or the tight, tidy, miniaturized madness of Chris Ware. Into the former category—the folly—we might put all the things that got Dr. Frederick Wertham so upset about EC Comics in the early fifties, the syringe-pierced eyeballs and baseball diamonds made from human organs; or the short-lived outfitting of certain Marvel titles in 1965 with a label that boasted "A Marvel Pop Art Production"; or the hypertrophied, tooth-gnashing, bloodletting quote-unquote heroes of the era that followed Miller's *The Dark Knight Returns*. An excess of the desire to appear grown up is one of the defining characteristics of adolescence. But these follies were the inevitable missteps and overreachings in the course of a campaign that was, in the end, successful.

Because the battle has now, in fact, been won. Not only are comics appealing to a wider and older audience than ever before, but the idea of comics as a valid art form on a par at least with, say, film or rock and roll is widely if not quite universally accepted. Comics and graphic novels are regularly reviewed and debated in *Entertainment Weekly*, the *New York Times Book Review*, even in the august pages of the *New York Review of Books*. Ben Katchor won a MacArthur Fellowship, and Art Spiegelman a Pulitzer Prize.

But the strange counterphenomenon to this indisputable rise in the reputation, the ambition, the sophistication, and the literary and artistic merit of many of our best comics over the past couple of decades, is that over roughly the same period comics readership has declined. Some adults are reading better comics than ever before; but fewer people overall are reading any—far fewer, certainly, than in the great sales heyday of the medium, the early fifties, when by some estimates[*] as many as 650 million comic books were sold annually (compared to somewhere in the neighborhood of 80 million today). The top ten best-selling comic books in 1996, primarily issues making up two limited series, Marvel's *Civil Wars* and DC's *Infinite Crisis*, were all superhero books, and, like the majority of superhero books in the post–*Dark Knight*, post-*Watchmen* era, all of them dealt rather grimly, and in the somewhat hand-wringing fashion that has become obligatory, with the undoubtedly grown-up issues of violence, freedom, terrorism, vigilantism, political repression, mass hysteria, and the ambivalent nature of heroism. Among the top ten best-selling titles in 1960 (with an aggregate circulation, for all comics, of 400 million) one finds not only the

---

[*] See, for example, www.comichron.com.

expected *Superman* and *Batman* (decidedly sans ambivalence) but *Mickey Mouse*, *Looney Tunes*, and the classic sagas of *Uncle Scrooge*. And nearly the whole of the list for that year, from top to bottom, through *Casper the Friendly Ghost* (#14) and *Little Archie* (#25) to *Felix the Cat* (#47), is made up of kids' stuff, more or less greasy.

To recap—Days when comics aimed were at kids: huge sales. Days when comics are aimed at adults: not so huge sales, and declining.

The situation is more complicated than that, of course. Since 1960 there have been fundamental changes in a lot of things, among them the way comics are produced, licensed, marketed, and distributed. But maybe it is not too surprising that for a while now, fundamental changes and all, some people have been wondering: what if there were comic books for children?

Leaving aside questions of creator's rights, paper costs, retail consolidation, the explosive growth of the collector market, and direct-market sales, a lot of comic-book people will tell you that there is simply too much competition for the kid dollar these days and that, thrown into the arena with video games, special-effects-laden films, the Internet, iPods, etc., comics will inevitably lose out. I find this argument unconvincing, not to mention a cop out. It is, furthermore, an example of our weird naïveté, in this generation, about how sophisticated we and our children have become vis-à-vis our parents and grandparents, of the misguided sense of retrospective superiority we tend to display toward them and their vanished world. As if in 1960 there was not a *ton* of cool stuff besides comic books on which a kid could spend his or her considerably less constricted time and considerably more limited funds. In the early days of comics, in fact, unlike now, a moderately adventuresome child could find all kinds of things to do that were not only fun (partly because they took place with no adult supervision or mediation), but absolutely free. The price of fun doesn't get any more competitive than that.

I also refuse to accept as explanation for anything the often-tendered argument that contemporary children are more sophisticated, that the kind of comics that pleased a seven-year-old in 1960 would leave an ultracool kid of today snickering with disdain. Even if we accept this argument with respect to "old-fashioned" comics, it would seem to be invalidated by the increasing sophistication of comic books over the past decades. But I reject its very premise. The supposed sophistication—a better term would be *knowingness*—of modern children is largely, I believe, a matter of style, a pose which they have adapted from and modeled on the rampant pose of knowingness, of being wised up, that characterizes the contemporary American style, and has done at least since the late fifties–early sixties heyday of *Mad* magazine (a publication largely enjoyed, from the beginning, by children). Even in their irony and cynicism there is something appealingly insincere, maladroit, and, well, *childish* about children. What is more, I have found that even my own children, as knowing as they often like to present themselves, still take profound pleasure in the old comics that I have given them to read. My older son has still not quite recovered from the heartbreak he felt, when he was seven, reading an old "archive edition" of *Legion of Superheroes*, at the tragic death of Ferro Lad.

Children did not abandon comics; comics, in their drive to attain respect and artistic accomplishment, abandoned children. And for a long time the lovers and partisans of comics were afraid, after so many years of struggle and hard work and incremental gains, to pick up that old jar of greasy kid stuff again, and risk undoing all the labor of so many geniuses and revolutionaries and ordinary, garden-variety artists. Comics have always been an arriviste art form, and all upstarts are to some degree ashamed of their beginnings. But shame, anxiety, the desire to preserve hard-won gains—such considerations no longer serve to explain the disappearance of children's comics. The truth is that comic-book creators have simply lost the habit of telling stories to children. And how sad is that?

When commentators on comics address this question, in the hope of encouraging publishers, writers, and artists to produce new comic books with children in mind, they usually try formulating some version of the following simple equation: create more child readers now, and you will find yourselves with more adult readers later on. Hook them early, in other words. But maybe the equation isn't so simple after all. Maybe what we need, given the sophistication of children (if we want to concede that point) and the competition for their attention and their disposable income (which has always been a factor), is not simply *more* comics for kids, but more *great* comics for kids.

Easy, I suppose, for me to say. So although I am certain that there are many professional creators of comics—people with a good ear and a sharp eye for and a natural understanding of children and their enthusiasms—who would be able to do a far better job of it, having thrown down the finned, skintight gauntlet, I now feel obliged to offer, at the least, a few tentative principles and one concrete suggestion on how more great comics for kids might be teased into the marketplace, even by amateurs like me. I have drawn these principles, in part, from my memories of the comics I loved when I was young, but I think they hold true as well for the best and most successful works of children's literature.

1) Let's not tell stories that we think "kids of today" might

like. That is a route to inevitable failure and possible loss of sanity. *We should tell stories that we would have liked as kids.* Twist endings, the unexpected usefulness of unlikely knowledge, nobility and bravery where it's least expected, and the sudden emergence of a thread of goodness in a wicked nature, those were the kind of stories told by the writers and artists of the comic books that I liked.

2) Let's tell stories that, over time, build up an intricate, involved, involving mythology that is also accessible and comprehensible at any point of entry. The *intricacy*, the accretion of lore over time, should be both inventive and familiar, founded in old mythologies and fears but fully reinterpreted, reimagined. It will demand, it will ache, to be mastered by a child's mythology-mastering imagination. The *accessibility* will come from our making a commitment to tell a full, complete story, or a complete piece of a story, in every issue. This kind of layering of intricate lore and narrative completeness was a hallmark of the great "Superman-family" books (*Adventure*, *Jimmy Olsen*, *Superboy*) under the editorship of Mort Weisinger.

3) Let's cultivate an unflagging readiness as storytellers to retell the same stories *with endless embellishment.* Anybody who thinks that kids get bored by hearing the same story over and over again has never spent time telling stories to kids. The key, as in baroque music, is repetition with *variation.* Again the Mort Weisinger–edited *Superman* books, written by unflagging storytellers like Edmond Hamilton and Otto Binder, were exemplary in this regard. The proliferation of theme and variation there verges, at times, on sheer, splendid madness.

4) Let's blow their little minds. A mind is not blown, in spite of whatever Hollywood seems to teach, merely by action sequences, things exploding, thrilling planetscapes, wild bursts of speed. Those are all good things; but a mind is blown when something

that you always feared but knew to be impossible turns out to be true; when the world turns out to be far vaster, far more marvelous or malevolent than you ever dreamed; when you get proof that everything is connected to everything else, that everything you know is wrong, that you are both the center of the universe and a tiny speck sailing off its nethermost edge.

So much for my principles: here is my concrete suggestion. If it seems a little obvious, or has already been tried and failed, then I apologize. But I cannot help noticing that in the world of children's *literature*, an overwhelming preponderance of stories are stories *about* children. The same is true of films for children: the central characters are nearly always a child, or a pair or group of children. Comic books, however, even those theoretically aimed at children, are almost always about adults or teenagers. Doesn't that strike you as odd? I suggest that a publisher should try putting out a truly thrilling, honestly observed and remembered, richly imagined, involved and yet narratively straight-forward comic book for children, *about children*.

My oldest son is ten now, and he likes comic books. In 1943, if you were a ten-year-old, you probably knew a dozen other kids your age who were into Captain Marvel and the Submariner and the Blue Beetle. When I was ten, in 1973, I knew three or four. But in his class, in his world, my son is all but unique; he's the only one he knows who reads them, studies them, seeks to master and be worthy of all the rapture and strangeness they still contain. Now, comic books are so important to me—I have thought, talked, and written about them so much—that if my son did not in fact like them, I think he would be obliged to loathe them. I have pretty much *forced* comics on my children. But those of us who grew up loving comic books can't afford to take this handcrafted, one-kid-at-a-time approach anymore. We have to sweep them up and carry them off on the flying carpets of story and pictures on which we ourselves, in entire generations, were borne aloft, on carpets woven by Curt Swan and Edmond Hamilton, Jack Kirby and Stan Lee, Chris Claremont and John Byrne. Those artists did it for us; we who make comics today have a solemn debt to pass it on, to weave bright carpets of our own. It's our duty, it's our opportunity, and I really do believe it will be our pleasure.

A page from an unpublished American Flagg!

THE KILLER HOOK
HOWARD CHAYKIN'S *AMERICAN FLAGG!*

1.

IN A POPULAR MEDIUM that needs to label everyone a journeyman hack or a flaming genius god—like the world of comic-book art—Howard Chaykin is something else: a craftsman, an artisan of pop.

I don't mean that Chaykin works harder on or takes greater pains with his drawing, though his panels and his layouts bear witness to the pains he takes (like many craftsmen he actually works rather fast). Nor do I mean merely that he brings deeper technical prowess to the comics page (though when it comes to page design, panel arrangement, line control, and the rendering of bodies, faces, clothing, streets, furniture, and interiors, his chops are matchless). Some of the genius gods of comic art, after all, have also been master draftsmen;[*] and one of the best things about popular media is that, within their capital- and calendar-driven confines, sometimes a hack, half by accident,

---

[*] Genius can get by, even flourish, with a limited artistic tool kit.

can turn out something haunting, dreamy, or beautiful. What I'm talking about is a kind—the toughest kind—of balancing act. Taking pains, working hard, not flaunting his or her chops so much as relying on them, the pop artisan teeters on a fine fulcrum between the stern, sell-the-product morality of the workhorse and the artist's urge to discover a pattern in, or derive a meaning from, the random facts of the world. Like those other postwar East Coast Jewish boys, Barry Levinson and Paul Simon, Chaykin, a man as gifted with a quicksilver intelligence, as irrepressible a sense of verbal play, and reservoirs of rage and humor of apparently equal depth, has spent most of his career seeking, and sometimes finding, that difficult equilibrium.

The pop artisan operates within the received formulas—gangster movie, radio-ready A-side, space opera—and then incorporates into the style, manner, and mood of the work bits and pieces derived from all the aesthetic moments he or she has ever fallen in love with in other movies or songs or novels, whether hackwork or genius (without regard for and sometimes without consciousness of any difference between the two): the bridge in a song by the Moonglows, a James Wong Howe camera angle, a Sabatini cannonade, a Stan Getz solo, the climax of *The Demolished Man*, a locomotive design by Raymond Loewy, a Shecky Greene routine. When it works, what you get is not a collection of references, quotes, allusions, and cribs but a whole, seamless thing, both familiar and new: a record of the consciousness that was busy falling in love with those moments in the first place. It's that filtering consciousness, coupled with the physical ability (or whatever it is) to flat-out play or sing or write or draw, that transforms the fragments and jetsam and familiar pieces into something fresh and unheard of. If that sounds a lot like what flaming genius gods are supposed to be up to, then here's a distinction: the pop artisan is always hoping that, in the end, the thing is going to fucking kill. He is haunted by a vision of pop perfection: heartbreaking beauty that moves units. The closest that Howard Chaykin has yet come to fulfilling that vision—though he has approached it many times—is probably still *American Flagg!*

2.

By 1982, the well-established science-fiction trope of a dystopian future America (or of a solar or galactic federation closely extrapolated from the American model), dominated by giant conglomerates, plastered with video screens and advertisements, awash in fetishized sex and sexualized commodities, fed and controlled and defined by pharmacology and violence, had been working its way into mainstream comic books for several years, particularly at Marvel. Just as Golden Age comic books had been influenced (and in some cases written) by the hacks and flaming geniuses of the slightly earlier Golden Age of science fiction, many of the creators of early-to-mid-seventies comic books showed the influence of sf's New Wave of the previous decade. The psychotic megacities and paranoid technoscapes pioneered in 1940s sf by Alfred Bester [†] (far ahead of his time and sadly neglected today), and further explored by Philip K. Dick, William S. Burroughs, Harlan Ellison, J. G. Ballard, Michael Moorcock, and John Brunner, were reflected in titles like Rich Buckler's *Deathlok the Demolisher*, Jim Starlin's *Warlock*, and the work, across many genres and titles, of Steve Gerber. Little by little, comics, along

---

[†] He wrote for comics, too, and is credited with creating the original Green Lantern Oath.

with the rest of us, began to surrender the old World's Fair–cum-
Jetsons vision of the way things were going to be. ‡

3.

By the time that Chaykin brought out *American Flagg!*, in
1982, therefore, the idea of a science-fiction comic book set in
a dystopian American future was not a new one; and most of
the fundamental elements of the world Chaykin depicts—earth
abandoned by its corporate rulers in favor of off-world colonies,
marauding gangs of armed motorcycle freaks, the city as a kind
of vast television or information screen that irradiates or medi-
cates its denizens with psychotropic sitcoms, could be traced
back to novels by the writers of the New Wave and their successors, to *Rollerball* and, of course, to *Blade Runner* (directed
by Ridley Scott, another pop artisan, and itself based on a Dick
novel), which premiered about a year before *American Flagg!* But
no one had ever crammed those elements all together before,
in quite the way that Chaykin did here: the post-nuclear, post-
global-collapse, post–Cold War, corporate-controlled, media-
overloaded, sex-driven, space-traveling, Jean-Paul-Gaultier-by-
way-of-Albert-Speer freak-o-rama that was to be life in 2031.

What Chaykin uniquely intuited, perhaps through the process
of adapting Bester in the early graphic novel *The Stars My Destination* (1979), was that with its fundamental liability to fragmentation, juxtaposition, and the layering of text and images; with
its multiple margins into which ever denser images and subtexts

---

‡ I don't think you can discount the influence of *Soylent Green* (1973) and, particularly
in the case of *AF!*, of *Rollerball* (1975), the first movie depiction of a future not merely
ruled but *styled* by evil corporations.

and submargins could be crammed; with its ability to hyperjump a million light-years out to the edge of the galaxy in the space of a quarter-inch gap between panels; with its mongrel vocabulary, its clandestine heritage of sex and violence, its nature as corporate-owned media outlet and mass-produced object; and above all with its accumulated history of stale, outmoded, and rotting bright futures, the comic book was perfectly suited not merely to adapting but in some measure to embodying the hybridized, trashy, garish future of simulacra and ad copy that comics had been hinting at over the past decade. Other comics creators had written or drawn the American dystopia; Howard Chaykin went and built one.

4.

I fear I have made reading *American Flagg!* sound like a grim, possibly even dreadful task. In fact from the first panel the strip, almost twenty-five years later, remains completely exhilarating. Part of the reason for this is the virtuoso display Chaykin puts on, with a certain vandalistic Brooklyn-boy glee, of how utterly to scramble the standard deck of page layouts that comic-book artists had been shuffling and reshuffling for years. Chaykin played, dazzlingly, with the effect you could get from just a handful of dull square subpanels arranged across a big single-panel page on which, in that one big panel, something violent and wild was taking place. All that gorgeous Caniffian line, putting the flutter into a lacy cuff, setting a gleam on the visor of a leather hat, flinging a spray of blood into the air, all that lavish, nonchalant beauty plastered over with Jewish gags, neon signs, talking-head nattering, tough-guy commentary, scientific annotation! If Chaykin's work comes squarely out of the tradition of comics art that likes to stand back and notice how pretty it is—a tradition that includes greats such as Alex Raymond, Mac Raboy, Jim Steranko, Barry Windsor-Smith, and Neal Adams—it is perhaps unique in that it also derives, less obviously, from another grand comics tradition from E. Segar to Al Capp to Kurtzman and the *Mad* men to Kyle Baker: the tradition of mocking wordplay, snide commentary, caricature, and the irrepressible, compulsive, sometimes perilous need to undercut more or less everything but especially comics art that likes to stand back and notice how pretty it is.

The characteristic Chaykin facial expression is the raised eyebrow—of irony, skepticism, puckishness, a satirist's rage. In his work, on his characters' faces, the raised eyebrow takes on an iconic power. It's a combination of punctuation mark, the line that indicates a flexing muscle, and the kind of ripple or wave that cartoonists use to suggest motion, explosion, velocity, shock. I have never seen a published photo of Chaykin in which he fails to sport one himself.

5.

People have been imitating, swiping from, and building on Chaykin's experiments in panel arrangement, text-balloon placement, and parallel narration for over two decades now and the thing still startles and disturbs the eye. It's like *Citizen Kane* in that way. Welles and Chaykin may not have invented or pioneered all the stylistic and technical innovations on display in their masterworks, but they were the first to put them all together in a way that changed how their successors thought about what they could, and had to, and wanted to do.

Citizen Kane remains an acknowledged influence on the movies and the comics that followed it. The debt to *American Flagg!*, while obvious, has been neglected. Its two great mid-'80s comics successors, Frank Miller's *The Dark Knight Returns* and *Watchmen* by Alan Moore and Dave Gibbons, are hard to imagine without its example; those two books in turn influenced much that followed. *American Flagg!*, in both its style and its concepts, fed the literary genre of cyberpunk that has since watered the entire landscape of popular culture, from comics and computer games to movies and television programs. Again, I'm not arguing that Chaykin invented dystopian comics or cyberpunk, only that he articulated a set of tropes and "packaged" them in a way that brought them to durable, ravishing life.

If *American Flagg!* were merely influential or innovative, its relative retreat from view in the past two decades would be more understandable; the same goes for its oft-remarked effectiveness as prophecy. Accurate prediction of the future, of its technologies and traumas, has always seemed to me to be the least interesting thing about science fiction. So Arthur C. Clarke predicted the global satellite network—so what? He also predicted the widespread use of hovercrafts and the dominance by 2001 of the commercial Earth-Moon space trade by Pan-Am Airlines (d. 1991). Such prescience or the obligation to display it is, more than bad writing, the element of a work of sf that most readily dooms it—regardless of whether the predictions turn out to be right or wrong. Every future we imagine is transformed inexorably into a part of our children's understanding of their past, of the assumptions their parents and grandparents could not help but make. If *American Flagg!* successfully predicted certain aspects of the hundred-ply world we live in now—and I think of it every time I see a lurid news headline about a pedophilic pop-star crawl under breaking footage of carnage or disaster, while a network meat-puppet intones the latest official spin—then that very success would condemn it to seem, in time, eternally passé.

It is not, ultimately, the brilliance of its technique or the aptness of the future it imagined that makes *American Flagg!* an enduring, necessary, and neglected pleasure, but the impeccable pop artisanship that produced it. So many of the purest pop masterpieces, from Michael Ritchie's *Smile* to Emmit Rhodes's self-titled first solo album, are neglected ones; even an acknowledged pop masterpiece like *Pet Sounds* has never quite shed its initial air of puzzlement-inducing letdown. *American Flagg!* has all the modern virtues that would seem to guarantee its place in the pantheon of seminal pop artifacts: irony, attitude, knowingness, cynicism, a familiarity with corruption and existential bad faith, a rapturous, at times hyperbolic sense of style, and that insatiable compulsion, mentioned earlier, to undercut. Its hero, Reuben Flagg, is not just a preening, self-regarding piece of beefcake—he's a redundant one, having been replaced, in his starring role on *Mark Thrust, Sexus Ranger*, by a hologram; and a self-conscious one. Nobody is more aware of the irony and implicit satire of his situation than Flagg. On the surface, he ought to be an ideal hero, and *American Flagg!* an ideal narrative, for our time.

But for all his cynicism and archness of eyebrow, Howard Chaykin, like so many pop artisans, draws the greatest part of his strength from the source that underlies all true visions of pop perfection: romance. Chaykin is, fundamentally, a romancer; "a storyteller," as the cliché has it, "in the grand tradition." Cynical, pompous or jaundiced, self-aware, embittered or corrupted, his heroes remain heroes, and the stories he tells never stray very far from their roots in Sabatini novels, *The Shadow* and *Doc Savage*, Chandler, Hammett, the films of Michael Curtiz. True friendship, true love, dying for a belief, self-sacrifice, even American ideals—such things, though he almost hates to admit it, are still possible in Chaykin's work. It's the instinct for popular narrative, for everything that Chaykin, in conversation, dismissively and affectionately terms "pulp," that guarantees Chaykin's status as a true pop artisan, neglect and all. But it's that deep ambivalence toward romance, the need to undercut, that brings a problematic wobble to all Chaykin's work. Like Paul Simon, who at once has felt and knows to be illusory the transcendent rapture of a killer hook, Chaykin's sense of romance and its conventions is always, at the same time, a sense of betrayal by them. In his earliest comics, drawing flashy, somewhat raw adaptations of Fritz Leiber's (already ironic) sword and sorcery tales, and creating short-lived titles such as *Iron Wolf* and *The Scorpion*, romance, the unabashed fabulating impulse of the storyteller, tended to win out. A cool head, quick reflexes, a steadfast purpose, and the love or memory of a good woman—along with that crucial Sabatinian "gift for laughter and a sense that the world was mad"—these were sufficient, or nearly so, to any challenge or evil the hero might encounter. In his recent work, although Chaykin's technique has attained the kind of effortless polish that, as with all experienced artists, is a synonym for correctly valuing his own strengths and weaknesses, the cynicism, the undercutting, the mockery, revisionism, and satire have tended to gain the upper hand.

American Flagg! stands at the glorious midpoint, at that difficult fulcrum between innocence and experience, romance and disillusion, adventure and satire, the unashamedly commercial and the purely aesthetic, between the stoned, rangy funkiness of the seventies and the digitized cool of the present day, between a time when outrage was a moral position and a time when it has become a way of life. Such balancing acts have always been the greatest feats of American popular art.

DARK ADVENTURE
ON CORMAC McCARTHY'S *THE ROAD*

1.

CHARLTON HESTON AND a savagely coiffed vixen, wrapped in animal skins, riding horseback along a desolate seashore, confronted by the spike-crowned ruin of the Statue of Liberty half-buried in the sand: everyone knows how the world ends. First radiation, plague, an asteroid, or some other cataclysm kills most of humankind. The remnants mutate, lapse into feudalism, or revert to prehistoric brutality. Old cults are revived with their knives and brutal gods, while tiny noble bands cling to the tatters of the lost civilization, preserving knowledge of machinery, agriculture, and the missionary position against some future renascence, and confronting their ancestors' legacy of greatness and destruction.

Ambivalence toward technology is the underlying theme, and thus we are accustomed to thinking of stories that depict the end of the world and its aftermath as essentially science fiction. These stories feel like science fiction too, because typically they deal with the changed nature of society in the wake of cataclysm, the strange new priesthoods, the caste systems of the genetically stable, the worshipers of techno-death, the rigid pastoral theocracies in which mutants and machinery are taboo, etc.; for inevitably these new societies mirror and comment upon our own. Science fiction has always been a powerful instrument of satire, and thus it is often the satirist's finger that pushes the button or releases the killer bug.

This may help to explain why the post-apocalyptic mode has long attracted writers not generally considered part of the science-fiction tradition. It's one of the few subgenres of science fiction, along with stories of the near future (also friendly to satirists), that may be safely attempted by a mainstream writer without incurring too much damage to his or her credentials for seriousness. The anti–science fiction prejudice among some readers and writers is so strong that in reviewing a work of science fiction by a mainstream author a charitable critic will often turn to words such as "parable" or "fable" to warm the author's bathwater a little, and it is an established fact that a preponderance of religious imagery or an avowed religious intent can go a long way toward mitigating the science-fictional taint, which also helps explain the appeal to mainstream writers such as Walker Percy of the post-apocalyptic story, whose themes of annihilation and re-creation are so easily indexed both to the last book of the New Testament and the first book of the Old. It's hard to imagine the author of *Love in the Ruins* writing a space opera.

There is also a strong current of conventional hard-edged naturalism at work in much post-apocalyptic science fiction that may further serve to draw and to reassure the mainstream writer. If the destruction is sufficiently great, life and its appurtenances are reduced to a finite set, mitigating the demand for baroque inventiveness imposed by other kinds of science fiction, while the extreme state of the natural world—global ice, global goo, global ocean—serves to reflect the extremes of human psychology, of grace under the ultimate pressure. The great British tradition of the post-disaster novel pioneered by M. P. Shiel's *The Purple Cloud* and John Collier's forgotten masterpiece *Tom's A-Cold*, retooled in the fifties by John Wyndham and John Christopher and brought to a kind of bleak perfection by J. G. Ballard in the early sixties, is very much a mainstream naturalist tradition, cold-eyed and unadorned, and novels like Christopher's *No Blade of Grass* and Wyndham's *The Day of the Triffids* were popular successes that found a wide readership. For the post-apocalyptic is also a mode into which mainstream readers may venture without risking the stain of geekdom.

The status of relative legitimacy enjoyed by the literature of global disaster may in part result from the fig leaf that a satiric or religious purpose provides, and from the congeniality to conventional realism of a world without supercomputers, starships, or eight-foot feline warriors from the planet Kzin. But perhaps it is mostly a measure of the growing sense in the minds of readers and writers alike, since the mid-twentieth century, of the plausibility, even the imminence, of the end of the world. Instantaneous global pandemics, melting ice caps, and transgenic eco-calamity have joined large-scale nuclear exchange as stalwarts of the front page of the daily newspaper. Meanwhile the old retro apocalypse is selling better than ever these days, reformulated in science-fictional packaging as the Left Behind novels.

Cormac McCarthy would have suffered no risk to his literary reputation and presented no insurmountable difficulty to his large mainstream readership, therefore, if he had written a science-fiction novel called *The Road* about a father and son making their painful way across the carbonized waste of a post-holocaust America. And it is possible to imagine his having written such a book. Though he is not known as a satirist, his *Blood Meridian*, about a ruthless band of bounty hunters looking for Indian scalps in Texas in the 1850s, can be read at least in part as a bloody pasquinade on the heroic literature of westward expansion. A pawky gallows humor is a reliable if underappreciated element in much of McCarthy's work, and in his only recent novel to be set more or less in the contemporary world, *No Country for Old Men*, about a man in southwest Texas running for his life after stealing millions of dollars from a drug cartel, there are strong hints of the outrage, disgust, and sense of ineluctable decline that drive the satirist. And for naturalism operating at the utmost extremes of the natural world and of human endurance, a McCarthy novel has no peer.

Indeed many reviewers, if they have not chosen to bestow on *The Road* the dispensation of calling it a fable or a parable, seem to have read *The Road* as the turn toward science fiction that any established literary writer may reasonably be permitted. "I'm always thrilled," wrote Alan Cheuse, emphasizing the novelty and, perhaps, the faint air of slumming that attends the notion of McCarthy's move to the science-fiction neighborhood, "when a fine writer of first-class fiction takes up the genre of science fiction and matches its possibilities with his or her own powers." "Part fable, part science fiction, total nightmare," said the reviewer in *USA Today*, having it both ways at once.

2.

In brief outline the relatively simple plot of *The Road* would seem to support such a reading. The book is set in the burned-over ruin of what appears to be the southeastern United States, ten years after a man-made disaster that is never specified has destroyed not only civilization and society but also, seemingly, every form of life apart from an unknown but small number of starving, brutalized, and miserable humans, and at least—perhaps at most—one dog. The universal wildfires resulting from the initial "long sheer of light and then a series of low concussions" have burned so intensely for so long that the resultant cloud of ash blots out sun and stars. The forests are forests of ash; the days are cold and cheerless and the nights frigid. The unnamed protagonist, whose thoughts are so often presented without third-person attribution that at times he verges asymptotically near to being the novel's narrator, spends his days trying to provide food, clothing, and warmth for his nameless son, who was born shortly after the disaster about ten years ago and has never known any world but this burned one.

Father and son travel south and east, toward the sea and what they hope will be a warmer climate. The father suffers from the respiratory ill-effects of a decade spent breathing ash and smoke, and is racked by spasms of bloody coughing that we understand from the first will eventually kill him. The son copes with the imperfectly understood and erratically imparted legacy of the past that he bears on his thin shoulders, attempting to reconcile the stories his father tells him with what is around him, to square the entire vanished culture and civilization implied by every word of American English that he speaks with the "cauterized terrain" of the unhistoried world he has inherited. It's a dead planet, and human corpses, grotesque and pitiful and vividly depicted, people it.

The travelers make their way, rolling an old shopping cart piled with their pitiful hoard of canned food and blankets down a melted interstate, cold, starving, endangered by every other human being whose path they cross. Before they reach the sea—which turns out to be no warmer or more congenial than anyplace else they have been—they regularly encounter scattered hanks of the living who remain on the depilated surface of the earth. With few exceptions these encounters are replete both with bleak violence and acute suspense for the reader. The eventual safety of a character in a McCarthy novel is always in doubt, but the reader's usual sense that a disembowelment or a clean shot to the brainpan lies only a paragraph away has never been so excruciating as in *The Road*, where the life of a child whose innocence is literally singular is threatened from the first paragraph of the novel.

As they travel the father feeds his son a story, the nearest that he can come to a creed or a reason to keep on going: he and his son are "carrying the fire." Of what this fire might consist he can never specify, but from this hopeful fiction or hopeless truth the boy seems to intuit a promise: that life will not always be thus; that it will improve, that beauty and purpose, sunlight and green plenty will return; in short, that everything is going to be "okay," a word which both characters endlessly repeat to each other, touching it compulsively like a sore place or a missing tooth. They are carrying the fire through a world destroyed by fire, and therefore—a leap of logic or faith that by the time the novel opens has become almost insurmountable for both of them—the boy must struggle on, so that he can be present at, or somehow contribute to, the eventual rebirth of the world.

For the father their life of constant motion, his intermittent good luck at finding provisions, and above all his long habit of seeing his boy as the only thing in the world worth saving and the saving of him as his only reason to live, have engendered a religious sense of mission with regard to his son that is inevitably defined as a greater salvation: it verges explicitly on the messianic. Apart from keeping his son's body and soul together, this redemption is the father's greatest preoccupation. But in the face of the bleakness and brutality of their lives his mission is difficult to sustain, and the father dies before he can see his son or the world redeemed.

Manifestly there is no reason to carry on, fire or not, through this "scabland," which McCarthy portrays as so utterly defoliated and sterilized—the greatest corpse of all—that the idea of hope itself comes to seem like a kind of doom. The boy's mother arrived early at this conclusion, killing herself when he was still a toddler. The impossibility of ever finding a home—literally, a place to live—is dramatized and proved by McCarthy in a poignant passage in which the travelers discover a miraculous backyard fallout shelter, intact, untouched, built by some unknown survivalist—and here is McCarthy's humor at absolute zero—who failed to survive. Here they find warmth, light, enough provisions to keep them healthy and fed for a very long time. Yet they cannot stay; the shelter has been built to withstand fallout and fire, but it is not secure against the depredations of men. It's too exposed, too easily uncovered, and after a few precious days of self-indulgence the travelers are obliged once again to move on.

In this impossible land the mother's choice is clearly the only sane one, and nothing that occurs in the course of the novel up to the death of the father argues against the suicide that, contemplating his gun and his pair of bullets (eventually reduced to one), he repeatedly ponders. And yet in the end he and his author can't bring themselves to pull the trigger. McCarthy is ensnared and his hell undone by the paradox that lies at the heart of every story of apocalypse. The only true account of the world after a disaster as nearly complete and as searing as the one McCarthy proposes, drawing heavily on the "nuclear winter" scenario first proposed by Carl Sagan and others, would be a book of blank pages, white as ash. But to annihilate the world in prose one must simultaneously write it into being. Thus even an act of stylistic denial as extreme as McCarthy's here—the densely foliated sentences of *Suttree* and *Blood Meridian*, teeming with allusion and inhabited by exotic nouns and rare adjectives, are burned away; the chapters and scenes broken down into fragments and rubble—remains, in spite of itself, an affirmation. The paradox of language undoing the death it deals animates every passage of the novel, as in this typical description:

> The country went from pine to liveoak and pine. Magnolias. Trees as dead as any. He picked up one of the heavy leaves and crushed it in his hand to powder and let the powder sift through his fingers.

Powder, dead; sure. But those words "liveoak," "pine," the somehow onomatopoeic splendor of "magnolia," still flower greenly in the mind before McCarthy crushes them, and that leaf, which, if ash, must weigh very little, still lies heavy against the father's hand.

The paradox in every part and sentence of the post-apocalyptic narrative—evoking even as it denies—is repeated as if fractally by *The Road* as a whole. The son has wearied of his father's stories of the past, of deeds of heroism and goodness, of the world that no longer exists—"Those stories are not true," he complains— but he has none of his own to offer. He leads an all but storyless existence in which meaning, motivation, and resolution have no place and nothing to do. And yet of course the only way McCarthy has of laying this tragic state before us is through storytelling, through craft and incident and a layered, tightly constructed narrative that partakes of the epic virtue it attempts to abnegate.

This paradox, like a brutal syllogism, leads McCarthy, almost, one senses, in spite of himself, to conclude *The Road* on a note of possible redemption that while moving and reassuring is prepared for neither by one's reading of his prior work nor, perhaps, by the novel itself. In order to destroy the world, it becomes necessary to save it.

3.

All the elements of a science-fiction novel of the post-apocalypse are present or at least hinted at, then, in *The Road*: the urgent naturalism of McCarthy's description of torched woodland, desiccated human remains, decaying structures, human and natural violence; the ambivalence toward technology embodied in the destructive-redemptive role of fire; the faint inventive echoes of works like Roger Zelazny's *Damnation Alley* and the *Mad Max* movies in McCarthy's "bloodcults," roving gangs of tattooed barbarian cannibals driven by lust and hunger and surviving bits of diesel-powered machinery; and the strong invitation to pardon the exercise as a fable extended by the namelessness of characters and locales, by the vague nature of the disaster that has befallen the world, by the presence of at least one semi-allegorical character, and the usual, inevitable (in McCarthy's work generally and the genre as a whole) speculation on the presence or absence of God. There are bits of satire of a very dark order in the hints that religious extremism caused this holocaust, and in the relentless way McCarthy deprives the foolish reader of the reassurances— a few precious surviving books, a luxuriant return of wildlife, a sense of savage freedom, or a necessary cleansing of the old corrupt world—of the strange comfort that post-apocalyptic stories characteristically provide.

The Road is most profitably read, however, neither as parable nor as science fiction, and fundamentally it marks not a departure from but a return to McCarthy's most brilliant genre work, combined in a manner we have not seen since *Blood Meridian*: adventure and Gothic horror. That book (also a western, of course, like its three successors) is usually viewed not only as McCarthy's greatest—a view I passionately share—but as representing a kind of fulcrum, a borderland between the early quartet of Tennessee novels written in the 1960s and '70s (*The Orchard Keeper*, *Outer Dark*, *Child of God*, and *Suttree*), which left McCarthy in obscurity, and the Border Trilogy (*All the Pretty Horses*, *The Crossing*, and *Cities of the Plain*), which brought him fame. In *Blood Meridian* lushness of prose counterbalances aridity of setting; digression and indirection have not yet ceded the narrative to the dictates of the trilogy's archetypal western plots; and the Gothic impulse vies fiercely with the call to adventure. Setting aside the halfhearted *No Country for Old Men*, as charitably even the lover of McCarthy must, *The Road* seems to work its way back to the rich storytelling borderland of horror and the epic.

It is the adventure story in both its modern and epic forms that structures the narrative. There are strong echoes of the Jack London–style adventure, down to this novel's thematic emphasis on the imperative to build a fire, in the father's inherent resourcefulness, in his handiness with tools and guns, his foresight and punctilio, his resolve—you can only call it pluck—in the face of overwhelming natural odds, savage tribesmen, and the despair of solitude. Of course the underlying model for this modern kind of adventure story is *Robinson Crusoe*; and post-apocalyptic tales of lone survivors, such as George R. Stewart's classic *Earth Abides*, have long played fruitfully with the pattern of Defoe's novel, depicting as heroic if problematic a lone attempt to impose a bourgeois social order on an irrational empty wilderness after the Bomb or virus strikes.

The Road can also be read as an older form of adventure story that became discredited after the advent of Robinson Crusoe, that orderly, bourgeois, house-proud, and anxious hero, but that has haunted the work of McCarthy for years: the epic. Like the earlier duo of John Grady Cole and Billy Parham, the two young ranchers in the Border Trilogy novels, *The Road*'s father and son—the latter's blond head evoked through conscious Grail imagery as a "golden chalice, good to house a god"—are bound up in a quest narrative, walking (by necessity, horses having become extinct) to find not revenge or justice or love as in those other books but a healing land of warmth and sunlight. There is no such place, we fear, and so, as in *Blood Meridian*, the quest here feels random, empty at its core; but the attitudes toward it of the characters and of the reader are altogether different. Though they and we fear it must end in tragedy and failure, we are rooting for them, pulling for them, from the first—and so, we suspect, is the author.

But it's not the goal of the journey, the movement toward healing, however illusory, that marks *The Road* as epic adventure: rather it's the passage of its heroes through Hell. In Walter M. Miller Jr.'s introduction to *Beyond Armageddon*, an anthology of post-apocalypse short stories, the late author of the seminal after-the-Bomb novel *A Canticle for Leibowitz* (set in McCarthy's Southwest) suggests that what most characterizes the form is not the setting or action—the scarred landscape, the savage contending tribes, the mutations, the deprivations, the desolation and death—but rather the epic persistence with which its protagonists are haunted by the ghosts of the dead, by the vanished. The world post-apocalypse is not Waterworld; it's the Underworld. In his stories, his memories, and above all in his dreams, the father in *The Road* is visited as poignantly and dreadfully as Odysseus or Aeneas by ghosts, by the gibbering shades of the former world that populate the gray, sunless hell he and his son are daily obliged to harrow.

Indeed the novel itself describes a course that seems to carry it into the ghost world of McCarthy's early novels and early life, abandoning the American Southwest, where the author has lived and has set his novels since the late seventies, for what seems to be Tennessee. At one point the travelers cross a bridge that may well be Knoxville's Henley Street Bridge, a talismanic structure in *Suttree*; at another they seem to repeat the visit that Cornelius Suttree, the hero of the novel who leaves his rich family to become a river fisherman, pays to his ruined childhood home.

4.

The constant haunting of the protagonist by the ghosts of his own and our collective American past marks the point where the strands of epic begin to blend, as in *Blood Meridian*, with those of the other genre in which Cormac McCarthy has to be accounted a secret master, and the rightful heir (but oh how one hates to invoke yet another Great American Writer in discussing McCarthy, who at times has seemed to be in danger of disappearing in a heavy snowfall of comparisons to Melville, Faulkner, O'Connor, Hemingway) to the American Gothic tradition of Poe and Lovecraft, dark god of Providence, Rhode Island, where McCarthy was born. McCarthy's early novels are not merely violent; they are almost gaudily so. They trade in necrophilia, perversion, and baby murder, and reading them one is struck repeatedly by the way he displays the bloody-minded glee of the horror writer, the gross-out artist, as when he goes to some length, in *Suttree*, to depict with atrocious vividness the slaughter of a hapless turtle to make soup; or, in this novel, notoriously, to treat readers to the sight of a baby roasting on a spit.

It is not enough for a horror writer to assert, with the mainstream of literature, that in the knowledge of death our life is vain show, and to set a skull as a memento mori in the corner of his canvas. No, the skull must have a starring role; it ought, as reported in one of the three epigraphs to *Blood Meridian*, to show "evidence of having been scalped." Better still if we see the neck tendons severed, the vertebrae snapped, and the skin flensed with a hunting knife or gnawed off the bone by clacking insects.

Horror grows impatient, rhetorically, with the Stoic fatalism of Ecclesiastes. That we are all going to die, that death mocks and cancels every one of our acts and attainments and every moment of our life histories, this knowledge is to storytelling what rust is to oxidation; the writer of horror holds with those who favor fire. The horror writer is not content to report on death as the universal system of human weather; he or she chases tornadoes. Horror is Stoicism with a taste for spectacle.

The end of the world, therefore, has long been a temptation as appealing to writers of horror fiction as to those of science fiction. Poe sent a fiery comet to do the job in "The Conversation of Eiros and Charmion." Richard Matheson, in his novel *I Am Legend*, sent a bacterial plague that induces vampirism, and in *The Stand* Matheson's greatest disciple, Stephen King, wiped out humanity with the superflu known as Captain Trips. And I think ultimately it is as a lyrical epic of horror that *The Road* is best understood.

Horror fiction proceeds, generally, by extending metaphors, by figuring human fears of mortality, corruption, and the loss of self. The haunted house (or planet), the case of demonic possession, the nightmare journey to or through a charnel house, the transmutation of human flesh into something awful and foul, the exposed wolfishness of men, the ineradicable ancestral curse of homicidal depravity—all of them tropes to be encountered, in one form or another, in McCarthy's work—trade on these deep-seated fears, these fundamental sources of panic, and seek to flay them, to lay them open, to drag them into the light.

What emerges most powerfully as one reads *The Road* is not a prognosticative or satirical warning about the future, or a timeless parable of a father's devotion to his son, or yet another McCarthyesque examination of the violent underpinnings of all social intercourse and the indifference of the cosmic jaw to the bloody morsel of humanity. *The Road* is not a record of fatherly fidelity; it is a testament to the abyss of a parent's greatest fears. The fear of leaving your child alone, of dying before your child has reached adulthood and learned to work the mechanisms and face the dangers of the world, or found a new partner to face them with. The fear of one day being obliged for your child's own good, for his peace and comfort, to do violence to him or even end his life. And, above all, the fear of knowing—as every parent fears— that you have left your children a world more damaged, more poisoned, more base and violent and cheerless and toxic, more doomed, than the one you inherited. It is in the audacity and single-mindedness with which *The Road* extends the metaphor of a father's guilt and heartbreak over abandoning his son to shift for himself in a ruined, friendless world that *The Road* finds its great power to move and horrify the reader.

THE OTHER JAMES

I'LL JUST COME RIGHT out and say it: M. R. James's ghost story "Oh, Whistle, and I'll Come to You, My Lad" is one of the finest short stories ever written. The problematic term in that last sentence, of course, is not "finest" but "short stories." It's a mark of how radically we have changed our ideas of what a short story, and in particular a fine one, ought to be, that there should be something odd about ranking this masterpiece of the Other James in the same league with, say, "The Real Thing" or "Four Meetings." The ghost story has been consigned to the ghetto of subgenre. Rare is the contemporary anthology of "best short stories of all time" that includes even a token example of the form.

Once it was not so. Once, you could argue, the ghost story *was* the genre itself. Balzac, Poe, de Maupassant, Kipling—most of the early inventors—wrote ghost stories as a matter of course, viewing them as a fundamental of the storyteller's craft. Edith Wharton was an enthusiast and master of the "subgenre"; her ghost stories are the cream of her short fiction. And Henry James himself, of course, gave us the one ghost story whose status as literature is not open to debate: "The Turn of the Screw." It was only the best of a good two dozen that he produced during the heyday of the form, in the latter half of the nineteenth century.

Maybe our taste has grown more refined, or our understanding of human psychology more subtle. Maybe we don't really believe in ghosts anymore. Or maybe for the past sixty years or so we've simply been cheating ourselves, we lovers of the short story, out of one of the genre's enduring pleasures.

A great ghost story is *all* psychology: in careful and accurate detail it presents 1) a state of perception, by no means rare in human experience, in which the impossible vies with the undeniable evidence of the senses; and 2) the range of emotions brought on by that perception. And then, by the quantum strangeness of literature, it somehow manages to engender these same emotions in the reader: the prickling nape, the racing heart, the sense of some person standing invisibly near. Everyone has felt such things, coming up the basement stairs with darkness at our backs, turning around at the sound of a footstep to find only an empty room. I once saw a face, intelligent and smiling, formed from the dappled shadow of a stucco ceiling in a Los Angeles bedroom. The face remained, perfectly visible to both my wife and me, until we finally turned out the light. The next morning it was gone. Afterward, no matter how we looked at the ceiling, in daylight or at night, the face failed to reappear. I have never to this day forgotten its mocking leer as it studied me.

It is tempting to say that, like his contemporaries Algernon Blackwood and Arthur Machen, Montague Rhodes James is something of a ghost himself, nowadays, at least in the United States. He haunts the pages of foxed anthologies with titles like *Classic Chilling Stories of Terror and Suspense*, his name lapsed into obscurity along with those of the authors of durable gems of the genre such as "The Beckoning Fair One" (Oliver Onions) and "The Monkey's Paw" (W. W. Jacobs). But in England he is still remembered, and even beloved. James is about as English as it is possible for an English writer to be. A hungry Anglophile, one with no interest whatever (if such a creature exists) in the ghosts that haunt old abbeys, dusty libraries, and the Saxon churches of leafy villages, could survive very happily on a steady diet of M. R. James. These are stories that venture to the limits of the human capacity for terror and revulsion, as it were, armed only with an umbrella and a very dry wit. They are still read aloud on the radio over there, in particular at Christmastime, when, as during the season that frames "The Turn of the Screw," it is apparently traditional to sit by a crackling yule fire and scare one's friends out of their wits. (And it would be hard to imagine anything more English than that.)

M. R. James presents a nearly unique instance in the history of supernatural literature—perhaps in the history of literature, period: he seems, for the entire duration of his life (1865–1936) to have considered himself the happiest of men. His biography, insofar as it has been written, is free of the usual writerly string of calamities and reversals, of intemperate behavior, self-destructive partnerings, critical lambasting, poverty, illness, bad luck. His childhood, though it sounds to modern ears to have been a tad heavy on devotional exercise, Christian study, and mindfulness of the sufferings of Jesus and his saints, was passed in material comfort and within the loving regard of his parents and older siblings; the candlelit gloom of the paternal church counterbalanced, if balance were needed, by ready access to the beauties of the East Anglian countryside that surrounded his father's rectory. His early school years were notable, if at all, only for the consistent excellence of his academic performance and for the popularity he attained among his fellow students, in part through a discovered knack for spinning a first-class frightening tale. At the age of fourteen he entered the world of Eton, and, though he spent the middle portion of his life as a laureate, fellow, and finally dean of King's College, Cambridge (itself a sister school to Eton), he never really left that sheltered, companionable green and gray world, assuming at last the mantle of provost of Eton in 1918, a position he held until he died. He was a brilliant, prize-winning, internationally known scholar of early Christian manuscripts who devoted his personal life to enlarging, slowly and knowledgeably, his circle of gentleman friends, a task made simpler by his brilliance, charm, wit, kindness, and affability. He took no interest in politics, involved his name in no controversy or cause, and traveled in comfort through Denmark, Sweden, France, and other tamer corners of the globe. The seeker after shadows who turns, in desperation, to discover what untold sufferings James, like H. C. Andersen or E. A. Poe, might have undergone for the love of a woman, will discover here a profound silence. James never married, and as far as we are allowed to determine, the complete absence of romantic attachments in his life caused him no pain or regret whatsoever.

And the childhood fascination with the tortures suffered by Christian martyrs, each date and gruesome detail of beheadings, immolations, and dismemberments lovingly memorized the way some boys memorize batting averages? And the spectral face at the garden gate, pale and wild-eyed and reeking of evil, that one evening peered back at the young James across the lawn as he looked out through the windows of the rectory? And the intimate eleven-year friendship with a man named McBryde, illustrator of some of James's best stories, traveling companion and inseparable confidant, whose rather late marriage, in 1903, was followed, scarcely a year later, by his untimely death? And the boys, the tens upon hundreds upon thousands of boys of Eton and King's, on whom James had lavished his great teacherly gifts, cut down in the battlefields of Belgium and France? And the empty lawns, deserted commons and dining halls, the utter desolation of Cambridge in 1918?

Over all of this speculation as to the origins of James's ghosts and horrors, over any hint of torment, shame, passion, remorse, or sorrow, the shutters have been drawn. The only evidence we have for the existence of such emotions in M. R. James is the disturbing tales he chose, over and over, to tell. Could they possibly be the work of a man whose life presented him with a nearly unbroken series of comfortable, satisfying, and gratifying days, from cradle to grave? Let us say that they could; let us stipulate that the stories are the work of a man whom life denied none of the fundamentals of mortal happiness. Violence, horror, grim retribution, the sudden revulsion of the soul—these things, then, are independent of happiness or suffering; a man who looks closely and carefully at life, whether pitiable as Poe or enviable as the provost of Eton, cannot fail to see them.

Along with A. E. Housman, Thomas Hardy, and even, we are told, Theodore Roosevelt, one of James's early admirers was the American horror writer H. P. Lovecraft (1890–1937). The two men shared a taste for old books and arcane manuscripts, for neglected museums and the libraries of obscure historical societies, and for ancient buildings, in particular those equipped with attics and crypts; they shared that requisite of any great writer of ghost stories: a hyperacute sense of the past. We all have this sixth human sense, to one degree or another, but in the case of Lovecraft and James the sense of the past is as evolved as the sense of smell in a professional *nez*. When it comes to their writing, however, Lovecraft and James could not differ more—in style, in scale, in temperament. Lovecraft's style is the despair of the lover of Lovecraft, at once shrill and vague, clotted, pedantic, hysterical, and sometimes out-and-out bad. James, on the other hand, writes the elegant English sentences, agile and reticent, that an excellent British education of his era both demanded and ensured. The contrast is particularly stark when it comes to their portrayal of the unportrayable. Lovecraft approaches Horror armed with adverbs, abstractions, and perhaps a too-heavy reliance on pseudopods and tentacles. James rarely does more than hint at the nature of his ghosts and apparitions, employing a few simple, select, revolting adjectives, summoning his ghosts into hideous, enduring life in the reader's mind in a bare sentence or two.

Evil, in Lovecraft, is universal, pervasive, and at least partially explicable in terms of notions such as Elder Races and blind idiot gods slobbering at the heart of creation. In James, Evil tends to have more of a local feel, somehow, assembling itself at times out of the most homely materials; and yet it remains, in the end, beyond any human explanation whatsoever. Evil is strangely rationalized in Lovecraft, irresistible but systematic; it can be sought, and found. In James it irrupts, is chanced upon, brushes against our lives irrevocably, often when we are looking in the other direction. But the chief difference between Lovecraft and James is one of temperament. Lovecraft, apart from a few spasmodic periods, including one in which he briefly married a Brooklyn Jew named Sonia Greene and formed a part of her salon, appears to have liked his own company best. He could be gloomy and testy, and was perhaps most appreciated by his friends at a distance, through his lively correspondence with them. M. R. James, on the other hand, was legendary for his conviviality, and loved nothing more than whiling away an afternoon over sherry and tobacco with his erudite friends. Indeed, friends—colleagues, companions—play an important role in James's stories, coming along to shore up the protagonist's courage at just the right moment, providing him with moral support, crucial information, or simply another soul with whom to share an unspeakable secret. In Lovecraft the protagonist has often cut himself off from his friends and companions, and must face the final moment of slithering truth alone.

Lovecraft wrote, in part, for money, often as little as one and a half cents a word; James was an avowed hobbyist of literature, and wrote many of his finest stories as Christmas entertainments of the sort already described, reading them aloud to his assembled friends by the light of a single candle. The stories are, nevertheless, unmistakably works of art, the products of a peculiar imagination, a moral sense at once keen and undogmatic, and an artist's scientific eye for shape and structure.

This brings us back to "Oh, Whistle, and I'll Come to You, My Lad," whose unlucky protagonist, Parkins, we first encounter in conversation with his fellow professors over dinner "in the hospitable hall of St. James's College." (James's stories never originate in cheap atmospherics, fogs or plagues or blasted landscapes, or with the creaky, dubious avowals of narratorial sanity so beloved of Lovecraft and Poe.) In the very first sentence[*] James displays the remarkable command that qualifies him as a great unrecognized master of point of view, which is the ultimate subject of any ghost story and, of course, of twentieth-century

---

[*] "'I suppose you will be getting away pretty soon, now Full term is over, Professor,' said a person not in the story to the Professor of Ontography, soon after they had sat down next to each other at a feast in the hospitable hall of St James's College."

literature itself. For the narrator, or the author, or some indeterminate, playful amalgam of the two, reveals himself before we are twenty words into the story, and will continue to remind us of his presence throughout, right up to the final paragraph, when at last he takes leave, with a strange kind of cheerful pity, of the shattered Professor Parkins.

I don't think any writer has handled a narrator in quite the same way as James in "Oh, Whistle." For the narrator here is not merely a disembodied authorial voice in the classic nineteenth-century manner. He is *involved* in the lives of the characters he describes, he *knows* them, he sees them on a regular basis—he is, albeit invisibly, a character in the story, cut from the same cloth, as it were, as Professors Parkins and Rogers and the rest of the St. James faculty. There are portions of the story, he suggests, that *could* be told, that actually happened—most of them having to do with the game of golf—but which he gratefully lacks the expertise to set down. This accords with a fundamental operation of the supernatural story, from "The Facts in the Case of M. Valdemar" to *The Blair Witch Project*, which is to make the explicit point—generally implicit or finessed in "literary" fiction—that what is being given is a *factual account*. All ghost stories are "true" stories. We love them, if we love them, from the depth and antiquity of our willingness to believe them.

M. R. James, more than any other writer, explores the wobble, the shimmer of uncertainty that results when quotation marks are placed around the word "true." Because at the same time that the narrator of "Oh, Whistle" is implicating himself in his story—scrupulously telling us what he has seen for himself and what parts of the story he has only heard second- or third-hand—his supremely "authoritative" voice and evident easy control over the materials establish him as unmistakably the *writer* of the story, its inventor, hurrying us past characters we need not overly attend to, rendering the events with an impossible familiarity. This, in turn, calls into question the fictional status of the narrator, and hence that of the author himself.

All of this, I know, sounds dubiously postmodern. And indeed James, not merely in his approach, at once careful and cavalier, to point of view, but also in fitting out his stories with the full apparatus of scholarly research (footnotes, learned quotations from Latin, references to obscure medieval tracts), often anticipates Borges and the postmodernists—and with every iota of their self-conscious playfulness. But the playfulness is worn so lightly, and the experiments in point of view are undertaken with such a practical purpose—scaring you—in mind, that even a critical reader may scarcely be aware of them the first time through. James is like some casual, gentleman tinkerer yoking a homemade antigravity drive to the derailleurs of his bicycle because he is tired of being late to church every Sunday.

"Oh, Whistle, and I'll Come to You, My Lad" is, in many ways, the prototypical M. R. James story. It presents a man who stumbles, through benevolent motives, upon a historical puzzle that cannot fail to interest him and, poking innocently around in it, inadvertently summons—more literally here than in other stories—an unexpected revenant of a bygone time, with frightful results. Professor Parkins—"rather hen-like, perhaps, in his little ways; totally destitute, alas! of the sense of humour, but at the same time dauntless and sincere in his convictions, and a man deserving of the greatest respect"—kindly agrees to take time away from his golfing vacation on the Suffolk coast in order to investigate the ruins, in the neighborhood where he plans to stay, of an old Knights Templar church in which one of his colleagues takes a scholarly interest. Parkins, we have seen, is an avowed skeptic when it comes to the supernatural—to a fault, perhaps. Digging with his pocketknife in the earth around the ruins, he uncovers a strange metal flute bearing an enigmatic Latin inscription. When—as inevitably he must—Parkins plays a few notes on the flute, he calls up a series of increasingly terrifying disturbances, both atmospheric and psychic: winds, night terrors, and puzzling disarrangements or disturbances of the second, supposedly empty bed in his room at the Globe Inn. These disturbances culminate in the awful apparition—a marvel of James's gift for creating horror through understatement and suggestion—of a thing, some thing, with a woeful face of crumpled bed linens.

For this story is also prototypical James in that when at last we encounter the Horror, there is something about its manifestation, its physical attributes, its *habits*, that puts the reader in mind, however reluctantly, of sex. I say reluctantly in part because the cool, fleshy, pink, protruberant, furred, toothed, or mouthed apparitions one finds in M. R. James are so loathsome; and in part because James keeps his stories studiously free— swept clean—not merely of references to sexual behavior but of all the hot-and-heavy metaphor and overt Freudian paraphernalia with which supernatural fiction is so often encumbered. James is a hospitable writer, and one wishes not to offend one's host. But the fact remains that "Oh, Whistle, and I'll Come to You, My Lad" is a story about a man pursued into the darkness of a strange bedroom, and all of the terror is ultimately generated by a vision of a horribly disordered bed. The bodily horror, the uncanny, even repulsive nature of sex—a favorite theme of the genre from Stoker to Cronenberg—is a recurring element in the stories of M. R. James, rendered all the more potent because it feels so genuinely *unconscious*. Sex was undoubtedly the last thing on the mind of M. R. James as he sat down to compose his Christmas creepers, but it is often the first thing to emerge when the stays of reality are loosened.

At times, as in traditional ghost stories (e.g., "A Christmas Carol"), James's characters engender and deserve their ghastly fates, bringing them about through excesses of ambition, pride, or greed. Professor Parkins, one senses, does not entirely meet with the author's approval—he is priggish, skeptical, he plays golf—but in other stories the protagonists are men whose profession, temperament, and tastes barely distinguish them from their creator. Most of the time they are innocents, ignorant trippers and travelers who brush up against the omnipresent meaningless malevolence of the world, and the sins for which they are punished tend, likely as not, to be virtues—curiosity, honesty, a sympathy for bygone eras, a desire to do honor to one's ancestors. And, often, their punishment is far grimmer than the scare that Professor Parkins receives.

The secret power of James's work lies in his steadfast refusal to explain fully, in the end, the mechanisms that have brought about the local irruption of Evil he describes, and yet to leave us, time and again, utterly convinced that such an explanation is possible, if only we were in possession of all the facts. He makes us *feel* the logic of haunting, the residue of some inscrutable chain of ghostly causation, though we can't—though, he insists, we *never will be able to*—explain or understand that logic. In "Oh, Whistle" the elements—the Templars' ruined church, the brass flute with its fragmentary inscriptions, the blind pursuing figure in white, the whistled-up wind—all hang together seamlessly in the reader's imagination: they fit. And yet, in the end, we have no idea why. For the central story of M. R. James, reiterated with inexhaustible inventiveness, is ultimately the breathtaking fragility of life, of "reality," of all the structures that we have erected to defend ourselves from our constant nagging suspicion that underlying everything is chaos, brutal and unreasoning. It is hard to conceive of a more serious theme, or a more contemporary plot, than this.

It may be, in fact, that the ghost story, like the dinosaur, is still very much with us, transformed past the point of ready recognition into the feathered thing that we call "the modern short story." Perhaps all short stories can be understood as ghost stories, accounts of visitations and reckonings with the traces of the past. Were there ever characters in fiction more haunted by ghosts than Chekhov's or Joyce's?

The short story narrates the moment when a dark door, long closed, is opened, when a forgotten error is unwittingly repeated, when the fabric of a life is revealed to have been woven from frail and dubious fiber over top of something unknowable and possibly very bad. Ultimately all stories—ghost stories, mysteries, stories of terror or adventure or modern urban life—descend from the fireside tale, told with wolves in the woods all around, with winter howling at the window. After centuries of the refinements, custom fittings, and mutations introduced by artistry and the marketplace, the short story retains its fundamental power to frighten us with its recognition of the abyss at our backs, and to warm us with its flickering light.

LANDSMAN OF THE LOST

L IKE MANY PEOPLE, I was first apprised of the wistful and intrepid pilgrimage of Mr. Julius Knipl by Lawrence Weschler, in his 1993 *New Yorker* profile of Ben Katchor, creator of the last great American comic strip.

It is a sad duty to thus anoint *Julius Knipl, Real Estate Photographer*. Perhaps no art form has ever flourished so brilliantly only to decline into such utter debasement, in such a brief period of time, as the newspaper strip. Reading the comics page in 1996, exactly one hundred years after the debut of Outcault's Yellow Kid, is, for those who still bother, half melancholy habit and half sentimental adherence to duty, a daily running up of a discredited flag in a forsaken outpost of an empire that collapsed.

Weschler's article dwelt at length, as do most comments on Katchor, on the artist's preoccupation with the sensuous residuum of the past, those unexpected revelators of the all-but-forgotten, encountered in the stairwell of a hard-luck office building or on the grimy shelves of a decrepit pharmacy, those stray remnants of

"The Remains of Dinner," page 45

an earlier time that are hinted at in the surname of his protagonist, the stoop-shouldered wanderer, meditative soul, and former
dance instructor Mr. Julius Knipl. And it is true that celebration
of the chance survival, the memory wrapped like a *knipl*, or nest
egg, in a beaded purse of forgetfulness discovered in the back of
a drawer, is the most immediately striking and perhaps the most
accessible aspect of the strip. It was this aspect, initially, that led
me to track down Katchor's first collection of strips, *Cheap Novelties*,
and—the spell was on me now—to take out a subscription to *Forward*, then the flagship paper of the scattershot and fluctuating
Knipl syndicate. I'm a sucker, myself, for such chance survivals,
because as I've confessed elsewhere I suffer intensely from bouts,
at times almost disabling, of a limitless, all-encompassing nostalgia, extending well back into the years before I was born.

The mass synthesis, marketing, and distribution of versions
and simulacra of an artificial past, perfected over the last thirty
years or so, has ruined the reputation and driven a fatal stake
through the heart of nostalgia. Those of us who cannot make it
from one end of a street to another without being momentarily
upended by some fragment of outmoded typography, curve of
chrome fender, or whiff of lavender hair oil from the pate of a
semiretired neighbor are compelled by the disrepute into which
nostalgia has fallen to mourn secretly the passing of a million
marvelous quotidian things.

The erasure of the past and its replacement by animatronic
replicas, politicians' narratives, and the fictions of advertisers,
coupled with the explosive proliferation of new inventions and
altered mores, ought to have produced a boom time for honest
mourners of the vanished. Instead we find ourselves haunting the
margins of a world loud with speculators in metal lunch boxes and
Barbie dolls, postmodernists, and retro-rockers, quietly regretting

the alternate chuckling and sighs of an old-style telephone when you dialed it. We are not, as our critics would claim, necessarily convinced that things were once better than they are now, nor that we ourselves, our parents, or our grandparents were happier "back then." We are simply like those savants in the Borges story who stumble upon certain objects and totems that turn out to be the random emanations and proofs of the existence of Tlön. The past is another planet; anyone ought to wonder, as we do, at any traces of it that turn up on this one.

Every week in the eight panels of a new installment of *Julius Knipl, Real Estate Photographer*, Ben Katchor manages to teleport the reader to a particular urban past—a crumbling, lunar cityscape of brick and wire which was young and raucous in the heyday of the Yellow Kid. It's a world of rumpled suits, fireproof office blocks with the date of their erection engraved on the pediment, transom windows, and harebrained if ingenious small businesses; a sleepless, hacking-cough, dyspeptic, masculine world the color of the stained lining of a hat. (This world, in its dreamlike, at times almost dadaistic particulars, may not ever, precisely, have existed; and yet a walk through the remaining grimy, unrenovated, simulacrum-free streets of any old American downtown, with their medical-supply showrooms, flophouses, theosophical book depositories, and 99-cent stores, can be a remarkably persuasive argument for the documentary force of Katchor's work.)

But Katchor is far more than a simple archaeologist of outmoded technologies and abandoned pastimes. In fact he often plays a kind of involuted Borgesian game with the entire notion of nostalgia itself, proving that one can feel nostalgia not only for times before one's own but, surprisingly, for things that never existed. Not content, or perhaps, in this age of debased nostalgia, too rigorous an artist to evoke merely the factual elements of a vanished past so easily appropriated by admen and Republican candidates, Katchor carefully devises a seemingly endess series of regrets, in the heart of Julius Knipl, for things not only gone or rapidly disappearing, such as paper straws and television aerials, but also wholly imaginary: the Vitaloper, the Directory of the Alimentary Canal, tapeworm sanctuaries, a once well-known brand of aerosol tranquilizer.

As, over the weeks, I joined Mr. Knipl in his peregrinations, I discovered that the strip's wonderful evocation of an entirely plausible and heartbreaking if only partly veracious past is not the greatest of its pleasures or achievements. Ben Katchor is an extremely clever, skillful, and amusing storyteller.

With the exception of mute strips such as *Henry* and *The Little King*, the comic strip is and has always been a literary form that braids words and pictures inextricably into a story. In the so-called Golden Age of the comic strip, standards for both elements were often high; lately the pictures have dwindled to a bare series of thumbnail sketches, and while the notion of story has atrophied almost to nonexistence, most of the burden of humor or pathos now falls, for better or worse, on the words. But we have never—at least not since Herriman—had a writer like Katchor.

His polished, terse, and versatile prose, capable, in a single sentence strung expertly from a rhythmic frame of captions, of running from graceful elegy to police-blotter declarative to Catskill belly rumble, lays down the bare-bones elements, the newspaper-lead essentials of his story. As in all great strips, Katchor's dialogue—the hybrid element unique to comics neither quite picture nor completely words—swelling perilously inside his crooked and deformed balloons, drives, embellishes, shanghais, and comments—generally ironically—on the story, his woebegone characters sometimes echoing the taciturn elegance of the captions, sometimes speaking in an entertaining mishmash of commercial travelers' argot, Lower East Side expostulations, and the sprung accents of cheap melodrama.

None of this would mean anything, however, without Katchor's artwork, running in perpetual counterpoint to and in tension with the captions and dialogue. Though his style in no way resembles that of either Jack Kirby or Will Eisner, Ben Katchor is along with them one of the three great depictors of New York City in the history of comics (Katchor's city, nameless or whatever its name may be, is always plainly New York). It is a dark, at times almost submarine city, with antecedents in sources as divergent as the work of Hopper, De Chirico, and Ditko. Wide, deserted streets find themselves hemmed in on all sides by carefully not-quite-anonymous buildings. Late-night cafeterias extrude wan panels of light onto the sidewalks. Lonely news vendors stand beside dolmens of unsold papers.

Katchor's style, like all the great styles, is addictive. His wobbly lines, woozy perspectives, and restless shifts in point of view; his intense exploitation of a narrow spectrum of ink washes running from soot to dirty rain; his use of detail at once lavish and superbly economical, painstaking, and apt; his lumbering, sad, hollow-eyed, jowly, blue-jawed men in their ill-fitting suits; his rare, mildly frightening women in their remarkable armor of trusses and lingerie—none of it is beautiful, or even, if I may be forgiven for saying so, masterly; the same could have been said about Herriman. In the funny papers a mastery of the vocabulary of comic drawing is more important than refinement of technique. Drawing skill matters only insofar as it helps the cartoonist tell his story.

The stories Katchor tells, mostly in eight or nine panels on a single page, occasionally spilling over onto two, three, or four pages (and wondrously, in the case of the longest and previously unpublished story in this collection, onto seventeen wild pages with an astonishing splash panel), fall, roughly, into seven categories. There are first of all the famous requiems for vanished places, sale items, novelties, and devices. There are episodes and accounts that serve to illuminate the ways and behaviors—from the Stasis Day Parade to the hazardous umbrella situation to the intricacies of Excursionist Drama—of the alternate Gotham in which Mr. Knipl makes his living. There are anecdotes and incidents taken from the lore of the local tradesmen, its hairstyle mappers, licensed expectorators, parked-car readers, and numerous cracked inventors. There are the odd, indirect, at times almost eventless stories so like dreams—the dreams beloved of readers of *The Evening Combinator*—that they linger and disturb. There are stories, inevitably but somehow incidentally, of Mr. Knipl himself, a lonely man in a city of lonely men, and stories of some of those other solitaires: Emmanuel Chirrup, Arthur Mammal, Carmine Delaps, Al Mooner.

In the end it isn't nostalgia but loneliness of an impossible beauty and profundity that is the great theme of Knipl. Katchor's city is a city of men who live alone in small apartments, tormented by memories, impracticable plans, stains on the ceiling. Small wonder, then, that they should so eagerly band together over and over again into the fantastic and prodigious array of clubs, brotherhoods, retirement communities, and secret societies, accounts of which make up the seventh category of Knipl story. "Fellowship," as a loyal member of the Holey Pocket League tells Mr. Knipl, "is the only thing we crave."

All seven of these typical narratives converge in "The Evening Combinator," through whose seventeen pages Katchor begins, not without regret presumably, to effect an evacuation from the blasted country of the newspaper strip to the rumored paradise of something known, a hundred years after a bald boy in a yellow nightdress first appeared in the lonely, teeming streets of New York City, as the graphic story. Interesting things are happening there; whether they ever reach the level of high quality combined with mass readership of the great comic strips—the creation of immense shared hallucinations—remains to be seen. Perhaps in a broken, nocturnal, past-haunted city of solitary wanderers and lunatic leagues, like this one, such universal fantasies and the fellowship they provide are no longer possible. No matter how we crave them.

THOUGHTS ON THE DEATH
OF WILL EISNER

BACK WHEN I was learning to love comic books, Will Eisner was God. Not God as in Eric Clapton—to be bowed down before, forehead to the ground, in a haze of dry ice and laser light. Gustave Flaubert once wrote in a letter that "An author in his book must be like God in the universe, present everywhere and visible nowhere." In 1975 Will Eisner was God like that to me. Some of the artists and writers of the day whose work I liked most—Neal Adams, Jim Steranko, Steve Gerber, Steve Ditko—had been directly influenced by Eisner, but I didn't know that. All I knew about Will Eisner was what I had read in Jules Feiffer's *The Great Comic Book Heroes*. In that book, by one of Eisner's protégés—a key work in the history of comics history—Feiffer passionately instructed the reader that Will Eisner was a genius and a pioneer, the one from whom all others stole and so forth. And I believed him. But I pretty much had to take Jules Feiffer's word for it. The eight-page Spirit story that Feiffer reprinted in his book—"The Jewel of Death"—remained for a long time the only full example of Eisner's work that I had ever seen. Eisner was out of print, out of comics. As a publisher, a packager, a talent scout, an impresario, and as an artist and writer, Will Eisner had created the world of comics as I knew it. But until I saw some of the later Warren (or maybe it was the Kitchen Sink) reprints, I really had no idea who he was or what he had done.

By the time I sat down to interview Will, in 1996, I was better educated. I had just started to write the novel that became *The Amazing Adventures of Kavalier & Clay*. A crucial part of my preparatory research was getting hold of all the Eisner I could find—the Spirit, the graphic novels, the books of comics theory—and the truth of Jules Feiffer's claims was obvious. Eisner brought radical technical innovations to the comics page—some borrowed from the movies, some from the theater, some from the fine-art tradition—and that was impressive and important. But the amazing thing about his Spirit work—all of Eisner's tricks and technical bravado, his wild angles and striking use of shadow—was how fresh and new it still looked, even after fifty years of constant imitation by peers, inferiors, and successors. A parallel can be drawn here to *Citizen Kane*, and to a certain extent Eisner and Welles stand as parallel figures in their respective media. Both of them were prodigiously gifted and managed at a young age to get their hands on a vehicle—a Hollywood studio, a newspaper syndicate—that would allow them to put on a dazzling display of those gifts. Both had a phenomenally sharp eye for talent in others, and the knack for yoking it to the service of their own schemes and ambitions. Both of them served as the secret and open inspiration, as touchstone and mark of comparison, for the generations of directors and comic-book artists who followed them. But Will Eisner had something—was something—that Orson Welles never quite managed, or permitted himself, or possessed a head hard enough to be: Will Eisner was a businessman. He was a Welles *and* a Selznick, a Brian Wilson and an Ahmet Ertegun. He was labor and management. He was the talent and the guy who had to fire the talent. Sometimes he signed the paychecks, and sometimes he was hanging on, himself, until the next one. He started companies, negotiated contracts, acquired rights, packaged material for sale. At the same time that he was practicing all that capitalism, he was dreaming and writing and drawing. He revolutionized an artistic medium, opened it up and theorized it and made it a superb vehicle for his memories, his emotions, his way of looking at the world. He had his failures, as an artist and as a businessman, because he took risks, as an artist and as a businessman.

Sometimes it's hard, trying to make art you know you can sell without feeling that you are selling it out. And then sometimes it's hard to sell the art that you have made honestly without regard to whether or not anyone will ever want to buy it. You hope to spend your life doing what you love and need and have been fitted by nature or God or your protein-package to do: write, draw, sing, tell stories. But you have to eat. Will Eisner knew that. He knew what it felt like to be hungry, to feel your foot graze against the cold hard bottom. He knew how lucky you were to be born with a talent that people would pay you to share. But he was also graced with the willingness (and, when he was lucky, the ability) to get people to pay a little bit more, to drive the price a little bit higher, to hold out for a better deal or a lower price from his suppliers. Will Eisner was a great artist and a skilled businessman; inextricably both. I loved that about him. More than fifty years after the first issues of *Blackhawk* and *Doll Man* and the other titles that he and his partner Jerry Iger packaged for Quality Comics had hit the newsstands, he still remembered the sales figures, the distributors' names, the dime-and-dollar details of hits and flops. And I sensed that all that stuff was every bit as interesting—every bit as important—to him as the nuance of an inked line, the meaning that could be compressed into and sprung from three square panels in a row. There may be many routes to happiness for a man; there may be only a few. But in his artistry and acumen—in the way he moved so comfortably through the world as an artist who worked for money and as a businessman who worked for art, I think that Will Eisner came awfully close to finding one of those routes. He was lucky like that.

MY BACK PAGES

I STARTED TO WRITE *The Mysteries of Pittsburgh* in April of 1985, in Ralph's room. Ralph was the Christian name of a man I never met, the previous owner of my mother's house on Colton Drive, in the Montclair District of Oakland, California. He had died, hit by a car while standing at the end of his driveway, shortly before his house was sold. I always pictured him as a stooped, soft-spoken man in a cardigan, scorned by the world, who retreated to his laboratory, where he turned into Ernest Thesiger and called wild Transylvanian lightning down from the skies. His so-called room was in fact a crawl space, twice as long as it was wide, and it was not very wide. It had a cement floor and a naked light bulb. It smelled like dirt, though not in a bad way—like soil and cold dust and bicycle grease. Most people would have used it for suitcases and tire chains and the lawn-darts set, but at some point this Ralph had built himself a big, high, bulky workbench in there. He built it of plywood and four-by-fours, with a surface that came level to the waist of a tall man standing. It might have been a fine workbench, but it made a lousy desk, which is how I used it.

I was living with my mother and my stepfather that spring, working as an assistant in my stepfather's optometry office and trying to get the hang of California. I had moved from Pittsburgh in December with the intention of applying to an MFA program out here. At the University of Pittsburgh I'd had three great writing teachers—Dennis Bartel, Eve Shelnutt, and Chuck Kinder—and of them Bartel had an MFA from UC Irvine and Kinder had studied writing at Stanford. Both gentlemen had said they would put in a good word for me at their respective alma maters. I'm sure Kinder did his best, but his effort could not avail, and in the end I found myself headed to UCI.

That winter I had been down to check out Irvine, whose writing program was staffed by a couple of novelists, Oakley Hall and MacDonald Harris. Of the seven first-year MFA candidates I met during my brief visit—they would of course be second-years when I showed up the next fall—all were at work on novels (three of which, by my count, were subsequently published—a pretty high rate). I rode the ferry and ate a frozen banana at Balboa Island, looked at the ocean, and wondered if Southern California would ever feel less strange to me, less of a place where people I would never know led lives I couldn't imagine, than Northern California did. There were lots of young women walking around in swimsuits and negligibly short pants and I suppose I probably wondered how many of them I would never get to sleep with. I was kind of on a losing streak with women at the time. I was in a bad way, actually. I was lonely and homesick. I missed Pittsburgh. I missed the friends I had made there, friends about whom I felt, with what strikes me now as a fair amount of drama-queenliness, that 1) I would never see them ever again on this side of the River Styx, and 2) they were indissolubly bound to me by chains of fire. My loneliness and homesickness were of intense interest to me at the time, as were young women in short pants, novels, and my eternal-yet-forever-lost friendships, and when I read a page of *Remembrance of Things Past* (as it was then known), the book that was my project for the year, I felt all those interests mesh like teeth with the teeth of Grammar and Style, and I would imagine myself, spasmodically, a writer. I hope you can infer from the above description that I was not yet twenty-two years old.

I returned to chill, gray Oakland from sunny Orange County, to the little basement room in my mother's house where I did some of my finest feeling lonely and homesick. There I ventured through a few more pages of *Swann's Way* and fretted about all those people I was soon going to be surrounded and taught by, people who were and knew themselves to be proud practitioners of novelism. Was everyone obliged to write a novel? Could I write a novel? Did I want to write a novel? What the hell was a novel anyway, when you came right down to it? A really, really, really long short story? I hoped so, because that was the only thing I knew for certain that I could manage, sort of, to write.

Now here I was, basically required by law, apparently, to start writing a goddamned novel, just because all of these windy people down at Irvine were unable to contain themselves. What kind of novel would I write? Had the time come to leave my current writing self behind?

The truth was that I had come to a rough patch in my understanding of what I wanted my writing to be. I was in a state of confusion. Over the past four years I had been struggling to find a way to accommodate my taste for the fiction I had been reading with the greatest pleasure for the better part of my life—fantasy, horror, crime, and science fiction—to the way that I had come to feel about the English language, which was that it and I seemed to have something going. Something (on my side at least) much closer to deep, passionate, physical and intellectual love than anything else I had ever experienced with a human up to that point. But when it came to the use of language, somehow, my verbal ambition and my ability felt hard to frame or fulfill within the context of traditional genre fiction. I had found some writers, such as J. G. Ballard, Italo Calvino, J. L. Borges, and Donald Barthelme, who wrote at the critical point of language, where vapor turns to starry plasma, and yet who worked, at least sometimes, in the terms and tropes of genre fiction. They all paid a price, however. The finer and more masterly their play with language, the less connected to the conventions of traditional, bourgeois narrative form—unified point of view, coherent causal sequence of events, linear structure, naturalistic presentation— their fiction seemed to become. Duly I had written my share of pseudo-Ballard, quasi-Calvino, and neo-Borges. I had fun doing it. But no matter how hard I tried, I couldn't stop preferring traditional, bourgeois narrative form.

I wanted to tell stories, the kind with set pieces and long descriptive passages, and "round" characters, and beginnings and middles and ends. And I wanted to instill—or rather I didn't want to lose—that quality, inherent in the best science fiction, that was sometimes called "the sense of wonder." If my subject matter couldn't do it—if I wasn't writing about people who sailed through neutron stars or harnessed suns together—then it was going to fall to my sentences themselves to open up the heads of my readers and decant into them enough crackling plasma to light up the eye sockets for a week. But I didn't want to write science fiction or a version of science fiction, some kind of pierced-and-tattooed, doctorate-holding, ironical stepchild of science fiction. I wanted to write something with reach. Welty and Faulkner started and ended in small towns in Mississippi but somehow managed to plant flags at the end of time and in the minds of readers around the world. A good science-fiction novel appeared to have an infinite reach—it could take you to the place where the universe bent back on itself—but somehow in the end it ended up being the shared passion of just you and that guy at the Record Graveyard on Forbes Avenue who was really into Hawkwind. I wasn't considering any actual, numerical readership here— I wasn't so bold. Rather I was thinking about the set of axioms that speculative fiction assumed, and how it was a set that seemed to narrow and refine and program its audience, like a protein that coded for a certain suite of traits. Most science fiction seemed to be written for people who already liked science fiction; I wanted to write stories for anyone, anywhere, living at any time in the history of the world. (Twenty-two, I was twenty-two!)

I paced around my room in the basement, back and forth past the bookcase where my stepfather kept the books he had bought and read in his own college days. All right, I told myself, take the practical side of things for a moment. Let's say that I did write a novel. Your basic, old-fashioned, here-and-now novel. Where would I write it? Novels took time, I assumed. They must require long hours of uninterrupted work. I needed a place where I could set up my computer and spread out and get my daily work done without distraction: Ralph's room. It had served Ralph as a room of his own, as a secret mountain laboratory; perhaps it would also serve me.

I lugged my computer in there and up onto the workbench. It was an Osborne 1a. I had bought it in 1983 for all that was left of my bar mitzvah money plus everything I had managed to save since. It was the size of a portable sewing machine in its molded plastic case, with two five-and-a-quarter-inch floppy disk drives, no hard drive, and 64 KB of memory. At twenty-five pounds you could shlep it onto an airplane and it would just barely fit under the seat in front of you. Its screen was glowing green and slightly smaller than a three-by-five index card. It ran the CP/M operating system and had come bundled with a fine word processing program called WordStar. It never crashed, and it never failed, and I loved it immoderately. But when I hoisted it onto the surface of Ralph's workbench, opened up one of the folding chairs that my mother stored in the crawl space, and sat down, I found that I could not reach its keys. Even standing up I could not reach the computer's fold-down keyboard without bending my forearms into contorted penguin flappers. So I dragged over the black steamer trunk my Aunt Gail had bequeathed to me at some point in her wanderings and set the folding chair on top of it. The four rubber caps of the chair's steel legs fit on the trunk's lid with absurd precision, without half an inch to spare at any corner. Then I mounted the chair. I fell off. I repositioned it, and mounted it again more gingerly. I found that if I held very still, typed very chastely, and never, ever, rocked back and forth, I would be fine. Now I just needed to figure out what novel I was going to write.

I went back out to my room and shambled irritably back and forth from the door that led to the hot tub to the door that went upstairs, mapping out the confines of my skull like the bear at the Pittsburgh Zoo. And my eye lighted on a relic of my stepfather's time at BU: *The Great Gatsby*.

The Great Gatsby had been the favorite novel of one of those afore-mentioned friends whom I had decided that, for reasons of emotional grandeur and self-poignance, I was doomed never to

meet up with again in this vale of tears. At his urging I had read it
a couple of years earlier, without incident or effect. Now I had the
sudden intuition that if I read it again, right now, this minute,
something important might result: it might change my life. Or
maybe there would be something in it that I could steal.

I lay on the bed, opened its cracked paper covers—it was an
old Scribner trade paperback, the edition whose cover looked like
it might have been one of old Ralph's wood-shop projects—and
this time *The Great Gatsby* read me. The mythographic cast of
my mind in that era, the ideas of friendship and self-invention
and problematic women, the sense, invoked so thrillingly in the
book's closing paragraphs, that the small, at times tawdry love-
sex-and-violence story of a few people could rehearse the entire
history of the United States of America from its founding vision
to the Black Sox scandal—*The Great Gatsby* did what every
necessary piece of fiction does as you pass though that fruitful
phase of your writing life: it made me want to do something just
like it.

I began to detect the germ of *The Mysteries of Pittsburgh*
as I finished Fitzgerald's masterpiece: I would write a novel
about friendship and its impossibility, about self-inventors and
dreamers of giant dreams, about problematic women and the
men who make them that way. I put the book back in its place
on the shelf and as I did so I noticed its immediate neighbor:
an old Meridian Books paperback edition of *Goodbye, Columbus*
by Philip Roth, the one with the lipstick-print-and-curly-script
cover art by Paul Bacon, a master of American jacket illustration
who would, in a few years, design a memorable cover for the
book I was urging out of myself that day. I had never read
Goodbye, Columbus, and as I got back into bed with it I remarked,
in its lyric and conversational style, its evocation of an Eastern

summer, its consciously hyperbolic presentation of the mythic Brenda Patimkin and her family of healthy, dumb, fruit-eating Jews, and its drawing of large American conclusions from small socio-erotic situations, how influenced Roth had clearly been by his own youthful reading of the Fitzgerald novel. That gave me encouragement; it made feel as if I were preparing to sail to Cathay along a route that had already proven passable and profitable for others.

There were two more crucial observations that came out of my reading of *Goodbye, Columbus* on the heels of *The Great Gatsby*. One was that Roth's book was a hell of a lot funnier than Fitzgerald's, which almost isn't funny at all, especially when, as in the famous Party-Guest Catalog, it tries its hardest to amuse. The second observation, of the most striking parallel between the two books, got me so excited, once I noticed it, that I rushed through the whole Mrs. Patimkin–finds-the-diaphragm sequence so that I could get up again and resume my caged-bear perambulations: both books, I noticed, coincided precisely with a summer.

This was a parallel both deeply resonant and lastingly useful. I had just been through, in the years preceding my decampment for the West, a pair of summers that had rattled my nerves and rocked my soul and shook my sense of self—but in a good way. I had drunk a lot, and smoked a lot, and listened to a ton of great music, and talked way too much about all of those activities and about talking about those activities. I had slept with one man whom I loved, and learned to love another man so much that it would never have occurred to me to want to sleep with him. I had seen things and gone places in and around Pittsburgh during those summers that had shocked the innocent, pale, freckled Fitzgerald who lived in the great blank Minnesota of my heart.

So there was that. At the same time, the act of shaping a novel as Fitzgerald and Roth had done, around a summer, provided an inherent dramatic structure in three acts:

I. June.

II. July.

III. August.

Each of those months had a different purpose and a distinctive nature in my mind, and in their irrevocable order they enacted a story that always began with a comedy of expectation and ended with a tragedy of remorse. All I would need to do was start at the beginning of June with high hopes and high-flying diction, and then work my way through the sex, drugs, and rock and roll to get to the oboes and bassoons of Labor Day weekend. And then maybe I would find some way, magically, really to say something about summer, about the idea of summer in America, something that great American poets of summertime like Ray Bradbury and Bruce Springsteen would have understood. Maybe, or maybe not. But at least I would be practicing the cardinal virtue that my teachers had so assiduously instilled: I would be writing about what I knew. No—I would be doing something finer than that. I would be writing about what I had known, once, but had since, in my sad and delectable state of fallenness, come to view as illusory.

I put Roth's book back on the shelf and went into Ralph's room and shut the door. I switched on the computer with its crackling little 4 MHz Zilog Z80A processor. I was cranked on summertime and the memory of summertime, on the friends who had worked so hard to become legends, on the records we listened to and the mistakes we made and the kind and mean things we did to one another. I slid a floppy disk into drive B. I paused. Was this really the kind of writer I was going to become? A writer under the influence of Fitzgerald and Roth, of books that took place in cities like Pittsburgh where people took moral instruction from the songs of Adam and the Ants? What about that sequence of stories I'd been planning about the astronomer Percival Lowell exploring the canals of Mars? What about the plan to do for romantic relationships what Calvino had done for the *urbis* in *Invisible Cities*? What about that famous sense of wonder, my animating principle, my motto and manual and standard MO? Was there room for that, the chance of that, along the banks of the Monongahela River? I took a deep breath, saw that I was properly balanced on my perch, and started to write—on a screen so small that you had to toggle two keys to see the end of every line—the passage that became this:

> It's the beginning of the summer and I'm standing in the lobby of a thousand-story grand hotel, where a bank of elevators a mile long and an endless red row of monkey attendants in gold braid wait to carry me up, up, up, through the suites of moguls, of spies, and of starlets; to rush me straight to the zeppelin mooring at the art-deco summit where they keep the huge dirigible of August tied up and bobbing in the high winds. On the way to the shining needle at the top I will wear a lot of neckties, I will buy five or six works of genius on 45 rpm, and perhaps too many times I will find myself looking at the snapped spine of a lemon wedge at the bottom of a drink.

I went on in this vein for several paragraphs, and some of what I wrote that first session ended up, after much revision, at the end of the novel, which I reached in the midwinter of 1987, in the back bedroom of a little house on Anade Avenue, on the Balboa

Peninsula, shortly before my twenty-fourth birthday. At some point that first evening, as with the help of Ralph's ghost, or of the muse who first made her presence known to me there in that room under the ground, with its smell of earth and old valises, I invoked the spirit and the feel and the groove of summers past, I did something foolish: I started rocking in my chair. Just a little bit, but it was too much. I rocked backward, fell off the trunk, hit my head on a steel shelf, and made a lot of noise. There was so much racket that my mother came to the top of the stairs and called out to ask if I was all right, and anyway, what was I doing down there?

I clambered back up from the floor, palpating the tender knot on my skull where the angel of writers, by way of warning welcome or harsh blessing, had just given me a mighty *zetz*. I hit the combination of keys that meant Save.

"I'm writing a novel," I told her.

DIVING INTO THE WRECK

I N 1987, IN THE final stages of work on my first novel, *The Mysteries of Pittsburgh*, I came upon a little picture that nearly ruined my life. It was a reproduction of an aerial painting of Washington, D.C., by the architectural visionary Léon Krier—a tiny prospect of blue water, white avenues, green promenades, glimpsed from a tantalizing distance, unattainable, ever receding. My reaction to this picture was strange: my heart began to pound, the hair on the back of my neck stood up, and I felt a sadness come over me, a powerful sense of loss, which I began at once to probe and develop, thinking that in an attempt to explain the inexplicable ache this little picture caused in my chest there might lie the matter of a second novel.

I didn't know that what I was feeling was a prefigurative pang of mourning for the next five years of my creative life.

I felt I had stumbled across a kind of treasure map to the barnacle-encrusted wreck of something true and important sunk deep inside of me, and I decided to try to bring it up and expose it to the light. Five years and some fifteen hundred pages later I was still trolling the murky waters of the Innermost Sea in search of that fabled wreck, which by then I was calling *Fountain City*. In that time I had found fantastic, shattered hulks and ruins down there, helmets and rimy flatware, chests of moldering silk, astrolabes, the skeletons of men and horses, but nothing that I felt could honestly be considered treasure. And when, at the end of 1992, with the help of my editor Doug Stumpf, I tried one last time to hoist the whole rotten caravel to the surface, it all just fell apart.

In the aftermath of this debacle, though I kept it to myself, I felt bewildered, depressed, and, to be honest, terrified. I was not accustomed to failure, nor to the bathyspheric pressures that weigh on a second novel, particularly where the first has met with any kind of success. The pressure I felt while writing *The Mysteries of Pittsburgh* had been entirely different in nature. I'd had no readers then, no book contract, no reputation, nothing but an MFA thesis to be written and a vague sense that in stringing together the seven thousand sentences of that thesis I was forging an identity for myself in the world as a novelist—or else failing abjectly to do so. It never occurred to me that if *Mysteries* didn't pan out I would be able to try again; I attempted to put into that book everything I had ever learned or felt, and to use every single word I knew. This purely internal pressure—to become, once and for all, a writer—was thrilling, astringent; it whetted the appetite, and I could feel myself succeeding in my ambition, or so I thought, with each new chapter I wrote. Most of the time the work, however slow or difficult, was also a hell of a lot of fun.

Writing *Fountain City*, on the other hand, was mostly no fun at all. Where *Mysteries* had been a kind of Drake's voyage, a wild jaunt in a trim ship to make marvelous discoveries and conduct raucous pirate raids on the great ports of American literature, *Fountain City* was more like the journey of Lewis and Clark, a long, often dismal tramp through a vast terrain in pursuit of a grand but fundamentally mistaken prize. Mosquitoes, sweltering heat, grave doubts, flawed maps—and, in my case, no Pacific Ocean at the end.

What was it about? This, unfortunately, is what I could never quite figure out—the great river of the West my large, well-equipped expedition never managed to find. It was a novel about utopian dreamers, ecological activists, an Israeli spy, a gargantuan Florida real estate deal, the education of an architect, the perfect baseball park, Paris, French cooking, and the crazy and ongoing dream of rebuilding the Great Temple in Jerusalem. It was about loss—lost paradises, lost cities, the loss of the Temple, the loss of a brother to AIDS; and the concomitant dream of Restoration or Rebuilding. It was also, naturally, a love story, an account of a love affair between a young American and a Parisian woman ten years his senior. The action was divided between Paris and the fictitious town of Fountain City, Florida. But I could never get those two halves to stick together convincingly, and I knew just enough about most of the above-mentioned subjects to be able to persuade the reader that they didn't all belong in the same book together.

So, at the beginning of 1993, after sixty-two months of more or less steady work and four drafts, each longer than the previous one, I dumped it. I didn't tell anyone, not even my wife, Ayelet, though unwittingly she provided the impetus that led me to leave that long-ago ache of architectural longing forever unexplained. We were living in San Francisco at the time, where Ayelet, then a practicing lawyer, was working as a clerk for a federal judge. She was due to take the California bar exam in July of that year, but one morning in January she announced that she didn't want to wait that long, and that, if I had no objection, she planned to register for the exam that was being given at the end of February—six weeks away. She felt she could be ready by then.

This came at the absolute lowest point in my years of work on *Fountain City*. Every night I went down to my computer in the room under our house on Twenty-Ninth Street and sat for hours, staring at the monitor, dreaming about all the other wonderful books I could have written in the last five years. On the day my wife told me she was going to be largely unavailable for the next six weeks, I went down to my office and found myself, inexplicably, imagining a scene. A straight-laced, troubled young man with a tendency toward melodrama was standing on a backyard lawn at night, holding a tiny winking Derringer to his temple, while on the porch of the nearby house a shaggy, pot-smoking, much older man, who had far more reason to want to die, watched him and tried to decide if what he was seeing was real or not. That was all I had, and yet it was so much more than I had started *Fountain City* with. I opened a new file and called it X. I started to write, and quickly found the voice of that shaggy old watcher in the shadows.

The first fifty pages wrote themselves in a matter of days. I said nothing to Ayelet or anyone else, but privately I had decided that I would take these six weeks of relative solitude and give this new thing, still in a file called X, a chance to grow. If nothing came of it, I would go back to *Fountain City*, having wasted only a month and half. What was a month and a half out of five years?

The new book seemed to want to take place in Pittsburgh, and thus, in my basement room, I returned to the true fountain city, the mysterious source of so many of my ideas. I didn't stop to think about what I was doing, whom it would interest, what my publisher and the critics would think of it, and, sweetest of all, I didn't give a single thought to what I was trying to say. I just wrote. I had characters. I had their story to tell. And, most important, I had the voice to tell it with. Six weeks later, after Ayelet had taken the bar exam, I took a deep breath and told her that while in all that time I'd done nothing to solve the problems of *Fountain City*, I did have 117 pages of a novel called *Wonder Boys*. She paled, then gave me her blessing. At the end of May, when she learned that she had passed the exam, I was two-thirds of the way finished with the first draft.

The hardest part of writing a novel is the contemplation of the distance to the end; and the hardest part of those five years I gave to *Fountain City* was that every time I contemplated that distance, it was never any shorter; or rather, no matter how close I came to it, I could never seem to arrive. There is no joy like the joy of finishing. "Harry finished the model of Fountain Field," I wrote of my apprentice architect in *Fountain City*, who is assigned to the building of a presentation model for a proposed ballpark,

> with a week to spare, at three o'clock in the morning. He took off his shirt and whirled it over his head like a lariat, assumed a soul-transporting Jackie Wilson falsetto, and switched from plain old skipping to the cool cool jerk. He jerked past closed office doors, slap, slap, slapping them with his bullwhip shirt. He cool-jerked into the foyer, made a reckless circuit of the receptionist's desk, banked steeply, and then set off across the drawing room once more. He played the drum solo from "Wipeout" on the drafting tables.

I wrote that passage somewhere in the middle of the fourth

year of that expedition, and you can see how thirsty I was. It almost makes me feel sorry for myself, this pathetic attempt to give myself a kind of false taste, four years in, of the sweet nectar of completion. But then I remind myself that if only I'd had more courage, I would have dumped *Fountain City* years before I ever reached this lamentable state. I would not have given a thought to the money I had already accepted, to the second-novel-savaging critics I imagined I was going to have to face, to the readers, however few or many of them there might be, who were expecting me to take them someplace worth going.

Six weeks after Ayelet passed the bar, I mailed the completed manuscript of a decent first draft of *Wonder Boys* to Mary Evans, my agent. Then I called her up and told her that I had finally finished my second novel. She said she was pleased, but I thought I could hear a faint note of weariness or wariness enter her voice at the thought of reading yet another interminable draft of *Fountain City*.

"There's just one thing you probably should know," I told her, and then, as I started to cool-jerk my way across my living room, I gave her the welcome news.

THE RECIPE FOR LIFE

THE BEST KNOWN—shaped from the clay of the River Moldau, by Rabbi Judah of Prague, to be a servant or protector of the ghetto—is the most dubious, having largely been devised and popularized by a series of novelists and filmmakers over the past hundred or so years. The most ancient is Adam, the original lump of earth into which, on the sixth day of creation, the inspiration of the Divine Name was breathed. But the story of the golem has a hundred variants, from the clay calf that was summoned to life and promptly eaten by two hungry rabbis, Hanina and Oshaya, in Babylonia two thousand years ago to such refinements as Frankenstein's golem of quilted corpses and Gepetto's wooden son. As I worked on my novel *The Amazing Adventures of Kavalier & Clay*, I discovered that its plot would require the famous Golem of Prague to play a small but crucial role. Once this surprising fact had become apparent to me, I went looking for information on golems, and found an insight into the nature of novel-writing itself.

All golem hunters inevitably end up at the feet of the brilliant Gershom Scholem, whose essay "The Idea of the Golem" (1965) probes dauntingly deep into the remote, at times abstruse sources of the enduring motif of the man of clay brought to life by enchantment. Enchantment, of course, is the work of language; of spell and spiel. A golem is brought to life by means of magic formulas, one word at a time. In some accounts, the animating Name of God is inscribed on the golem's forehead; in others, the Name is written on a tablet and tucked under the blank gray tongue of the golem. Sometimes the magical word is the Hebrew word for truth, *emet*; to kill the golem, in this case—to inactivate him—you must erase the initial letter aleph from his brow, leaving only *met*: dead.

There is good reason, in Scholem's view, to believe that some accounts of the making of golems are factual. Certain rabbis and adepts during the medieval heyday of kabbalah—those who long pondered the *Sefer Yetsirah*, or Book of Creation—culminated their studies and proved their aptitude at enchantment by actually making a golem. There were specific guidelines and rituals—recipes, as it were, for golem making. The rabbis did not expect to get a tireless servant, or even a square meal, out of these trials. The ritual itself was the point of the exercise; performing it—reciting long series of complicated alphabetic permutations while walking in circles around the slumbering lump of clay—would induce a kind of ecstatic state, as the adept assumed a privilege ordinarily reserved for God alone: the making of a world. It was analogical magic: as the kabbalist is to God, so is a golem to all creation: a model, a miniature replica, a mirror—like the novel—of the world.

Much of the enduring power of the golem story stems from its ready, if romantic, analogy to the artist's relation to his or her work. And over the years it has attracted many writers who have seen the metaphorical possibilities in it. On the surface, the analogy may seem facile. The idea of the novelist as the little God of his creation—*présent partout et visible nulle part*—is a key tenet of the traditional novelist, one that Robert Coover explored and exploded once and for all, it might have been thought, in his *The Universal Baseball Association, Inc., J. Henry Waugh, Prop.* But what gripped me, as I read and reread Scholem's essay, was not the metaphor or allegory of the nature of making golems and novels, but that of the consequences thereof.

"Golem-making is dangerous," Scholem writes. "Like all major creation it endangers the life of the creator—the source of danger, however, is not the golem… but the man himself." From the golem that grew so large that it collapsed, killing a certain Rabbi Elijah in Poland, to Frankenstein's monster, golems frequently end by threatening or even taking the lives of their creators.

When I read these words I saw at once a connection to my own work. Anything good that I have written has, at some point during its composition, left me feeling uneasy and afraid. It has seemed, for a moment at least, to put me at risk.

Of course there have been and remain writers for whom the act of writing a novel or poem is fatal, whose words are used to condemn and to crush them. In the former Soviet Union I met writers who once had to weigh every word they wrote for its inherent power to destroy them; during my stay I was reading the stories of Isaac Babel, imprisoned and executed not only for his words but also, according to Lionel Trilling, for his silence. Compared to the fate of a Babel, the danger I have courted in my own writing hardly seems worthy of the name.

For me—a lucky man living in a lucky time in the luckiest

country in the world*—it always seems to come down to a question of exposure. As Scholem writes, "The danger is not that the golem... will develop overwhelming powers; it lies in the tension which the creative process arouses in the creator himself." Sometimes I fear to write, even in fictional form, about things that really happened to me, about things that I really did, or about the numerous unattractive, cruel, or embarrassing thoughts that I have at one time or another entertained. Just as often, I find myself writing about disturbing or socially questionable acts and states of mind that have no real basis in my life at all, but which, I am afraid, people will quite naturally attribute to me when they read what I have written. Even if I assume that readers will be charitable enough to absolve me from personally having done or thought such things—itself a dubious assumption, given my own reprehensible tendency as a reader to see autobiography in the purest of fictions—the mere fact that I could even imagine someone's having done or thought them, whispers my fear, is damning in itself.

When I wrote *The Mysteries of Pittsburgh*, I feared—correctly, as it turned out—that people would think, reading the novel, that its author was gay. In part it was a fear of being misunderstood, misjudged, but in my apprehension there was a fairly healthy component of plain old homophobia—and the fear of homophobia. Turning in, to the Irvine writers' workshop where I was working on my MFA, the portion of the novel containing a brief but vivid love scene between two men, remains one of the scariest moments of my life as a writer. In *Wonder Boys*, I presented a character whose feelings of envy, failure, and corroded romanticism, not to mention heavy reliance on marijuana to get the words flowing,

---

* This line was written in the fall of 2000; I ought to have knocked wood.

seemed likely to amount, in the view of readers, to a less than appealing self-portrait. Again, my fears proved well founded: on my recent northern European tour, the first question out of one interviewer's mouth was: "Your Grady Tripp is full of drugs and having sex with many women. Mr. Chabon, how about you?" And there was the writing of "Green's Book." This story, of a man whose relations with his young daughter have been gravely damaged by his lingering guilt and shame over a childhood incident of babysitting gone awry, took me years to finish, so troubled was I by the conclusions I felt it might lead readers to come to about my own past and my behavior as a father.

Since reading "The Idea of the Golem," I have come to see this fear, this sense of my own imperilment by my creations, as not only an inevitable, necessary part of writing fiction but a virtual guarantor, insofar as such a thing is possible, of the power of my work: as a sign that I am on the right track, that I am following the recipe correctly, speaking the proper spells. Literature, like magic, has always been about the handling of secrets, about the pain, the destruction, and the marvelous liberation that can result when they are revealed. Telling the truth when the truth matters most is almost always a frightening prospect. If a writer doesn't give away secrets, his own or those of the people he loves; if she doesn't court disapproval, reproach, and general wrath, whether of friends, family, or party apparatchiks; if the writer submits his work to an internal censor long before anyone else can get their hands on it, the result is pallid, inanimate, a lump of earth. The adept handles the rich material, the rank river clay, and diligently intones his alphabetical spells, knowing full well the history of golems: how they break free of their creators, grow to unmanageable size and power, refuse to be controlled. In the same way, the writer shapes his story, flecked like river clay with the grit of experience and rank with the smell of human life, heedless of the danger to himself, eager to show his powers, to celebrate his mastery, to bring into being a little world that, like God's, is at once terribly imperfect and filled with astonishing life.

IMAGINARY HOMELANDS

1.

I WRITE FROM the place I live: in exile.

It's no big deal; certainly it can't compare to the exile endured by writers in literal flight from persecution, repression, intoler-ance, or war.

I write in a language of empire, the vital, burgeoning mother tongue of 350 million other people around the world. No regime or censor stands between me and the publication of my work—nothing but my own shortcomings and the invisible hand of the marketplace.

The circumstances of my life have always been comfortable, my freedoms guaranteed. I have never known anything resembling in the slightest the anti-Semitism that exiled my grandparents and great-grandparents, with no hope (and by 1945 no possibility) of return, from lands in which my ancestors had lived for a thousand years. If I want to return to the town where I grew up, all I need is a driver's license, a car, and money for gas. I bear no marks or scars. I haven't lost anything that isn't lost by everyone.

And yet here I am—here I have always been, for as long as I can remember knowing anything about myself—feeling like a stranger.

For a long time now I've been busy, in my life and in my work, with a pair of ongoing, overarching investigations: into my heritage—rights and privileges, duties and burdens—as a Jew and as a teller of Jewish stories; and into my heritage as a lover of genre fiction. In all those years of lighting candles on Friday night and baking triangular cookies for Purim with my children and muddling through another doomed autumn trying to atone, years spent writing novels and stories about golems and the Jewish roots of American superhero comic books, Sherlock Holmes and the Holocaust, medieval Jewish freebooters, Passover Seders attended by protégés of forgotten Lovecraftian horror writers, years of writing essays, memoirs, and nervous manifestos about genre fiction or Jewishness— I failed to notice what now seems clear, namely that there was really only one investigation all along. One search, with a sole objective: a home, a world to call my own.

2.

I am an American, of course—what else?—but the America in which I feel at home is only a kind of planetarium show, sound and light, shifting images projected by an inner Zeiss against the cranial dome. Quartered in my head, a slick media organ produces and distributes to an audience of one an ongoing series of specials, features, potted histories, and theme-park rides that retail (panning slowly from left to right across still photographs or rocketing me along in my little tram car) an ongoing saga of violence, delusion, innovation, and struggle in which heroes, eccentrics, liars, bad men, victims, bloodthirsty prophets of God—the audioanimatronic ghosts of Charles Manson, Jesse James, Satchel Paige, Robert Oppenheimer, John Brown, Harry Houdini, Kurt Cobain, the girls of the Triangle Shirtwaist Factory—suffer without flagging their clockwork torments or propound their visions in THX sound. At times it's a narrative as horrific as *Blood Meridian*, but like that novel one that is unable to rid itself, ultimately, of a final underlying tinge of romance.

Maybe everybody feels the sense of blinking disorientation I feel when I exit the turnstile of my own private Americaland and confront, say, the refrigerator hum, furtive faces, and doped-phosphor light of a 7-Eleven on a sketchy corner of Telegraph Avenue at midnight, walking through the door marked to gauge my approximate height in case I decide to hold the place up. I don't know. Maybe that strangeness is a universal condition among Americans, if not in fact a prerequisite for citizenship. At any rate it is impossible to live intelligently as a member of a minority group in a nation that was founded every bit as firmly on enslavement and butchery as on ideals of liberty and brotherhood and not feel, at least every once in a while, that you can no more take for granted the continued tolerance of your existence here than you ought take the prosperity or freedom you enjoy. I guess every American Jew has a moment at which he or she feels the bottom drop out, and I would be willing to bet that for many of us it comes when we encounter some testimony to the pride, patriotism, and fierce sense of national identity—of being at home—felt by the majority of German Jews in the years running up to Nuremberg. For me that vertiginous moment came when I read, in W. G. Sebald's *The Emigrants*, about a

Jewish congregation in Augsburg that voluntarily stripped the copper roof from its synagogue and donated the metal to the German war effort during World War I. That act goes beyond any demonstration of wild, heartfelt patriotism I can imagine from even the most loyally American congregation of Jews.

Twenty years later, on *Kristallnacht*, the Augsburg synagogue was burned to its foundation.

3.

I fear that these reflections on home and belonging bring me inevitably to the question of Israel. Israel, or a place more or less coextensive with Israel as we know it, is supposed to be my home—spiritually and in physical fact. Around the time of the first Babylonian Exile the primordial engineers of Judaism began to wire a longing for Jerusalem, for the restoration of the Temple and the sovereignty of Jews over Israel, into the core circuitry of the religion. Certain venerable texts have long been interpreted as indicating not only that the land belongs to me by right but also that more than I want or am capable of wanting anything else in the world, I should want to live there. If I remain unpersuaded by these arguments, then there is the less venerable but better reasoned argument of Zionism, which even before the Holocaust lent its awful weight managed to persuade and finally convince generations of Jews, among them large numbers of my Litvak cousins, reputed to be among the most skeptical, hardheaded, and unsentimental people ever to look askance at the productions and dreams of their fellow humans. That argument, reduced to its essence, runs like this: history has proven that we will never be happy or safe, never be able to fulfill ourselves as a people, without a country of our own. It is a European argument, as Milan Kundera has observed, first made by Europeans, calculated and calibrated with nineteenth-century European logarithms of nation and homeland. It has nothing to do with the claims advanced by those old texts inked with pain and longing on the skins of sheep, but an appeal to legendary ancestry, to the legitimizing claims made by stories of blood and soil and kings, was a crucial part of the nineteenth-century nationalist package. Nonetheless in the early days of Zionism there were vocal factions agitating for any homeland at all, anywhere—Africa, Australia, any place where nobody would mind, or notice, or care. Such a place was as imaginary in its way as the Promised Land itself, and has in fact never since been located. In any case Uganda had no hold on the imagination of the Jews. Every year for a thousand years or more, we had ended our Passover seders with the promise or threat or rueful wish or bitter jest, "Next year in Jerusalem." But under the pall of 1948 those words sounded, to the world, like a plan.

For millions of Jews living in the United States of America in 1948 and on every Passover thereafter, those four words proved troublesome, puzzling, even a source of embarrassment. What, I used to wonder when I was a kid, did they mean? Why did we say them? Were we, in fact, going to be in Jerusalem next year? We had said the same thing last year, as I recalled, and yet here we were again around my grandparents' table in Silver Spring, Maryland, making this empty and peculiar boast. In fact we had no intention, as I eventually realized, of packing up and moving to Israel. We were happy where we were. We were like the family that buys a summerhouse amid jubilance and great expectations, but finds it too much trouble to decamp there every year when it's so far and the weather is so fine at home. Or perhaps it would be more accurate to say that we thought of

Israel as our fallout shelter, to be inhabited only in the event of terrible catastrophe.

After many years, and during a time of relative peace between intifadas, I finally visited Israel, though not at Passover. I plunged deep into the history of the Jews and of my wife's family (she was born there), meeting cousins and mythical figures and old comrades-in-arms of my wife's father. My wife and I drove all over the place, from the Golan Heights to Eilat, sampling the food, viewing the cruel wonders of the desert and of the Romans, and marveling at the astonishing range of Jews on display. Like all Jews I was by nature and inclination an inveterate and passionate student of our typologies, but in Israel I felt like a lifelong birder of the austere tundra let loose in the Amazon and dazzled by its profusions. But I did not experience the stereotypical moment of endogamous rapture reported by so many Jewish visitors to Israel, the stunned encounter with a world peopled entirely by Jewish postmen, Jewish cops, Jewish cab drivers, Jewish junkies and punks, Jewish pedophiles and the Jewish prosecutors who sent them away to prisons guarded by Jewish screws. For one thing I saw Arabs everywhere, heard Arabic spoken in cafés and on the street and in the desert by Bedouins, visited vast cool mosques where pigeons wheeled high among the shadows and the arches. Every morning in Jerusalem we were awakened by the melismatic call of the muezzin. So all right, I'm perverse; it was the Arab side of Israel that I loved. Or rather I loved the imperfection of the joint between Jewish and Arab, the patches in the fabric where the reverse showed through. I loved it; but God knows I didn't feel I had come home. I love France and England too, and as with those countries I consider my culture, my history, and the language I speak every day to be vitally bound up with Israel's. When I left, I felt that I would like to visit again, and that I would continue to take an interest, even an intense interest, in the history and the look and the weather and the fate of the place. And then I would return to the theme park in my brain.

4.

It was soon after I returned from this trip to Israel that I first encount-ered a little book called *Say It in Yiddish*, edited by Beatrice and Uriel Weinrich. I got it new, in 1993, but the book was originally brought out in 1958. It was part of a series: the Dover "Say It" books: *Say It in Swahili*, *Say It in Hindi*, *Say It in Serbo-Croatian*. When I first came across *Say It in Yiddish*, on a shelf in a big chain store in Orange County, California, I couldn't quite believe that it was real. There was only one copy of it, buried in the languages section at the bottom of the alphabet. It was like a book in a story by Borges, unique, inexplicable, possibly a hoax. The first thing that really struck me about it was, paradoxically, its unremarkableness, the conventional terms with which *Say It in Yiddish* advertised itself on its cover. "No other PHRASE BOOK FOR TRAVELERS," it claimed, "contains all these essential features." It boasted of "Over 1,600 up-to-date practical entries" (up-to-date!), "easy pronunciation transcription," and a "sturdy binding—pages will not fall out."

Inside, *Say It in Yiddish* delivered admirably on all the bland promises made by the cover. Virtually every eventuality, calamity, chance, or circumstance, apart from the amorous, that could possibly befall the traveler was covered, under general rubrics like "Shopping," "Barber Shop and Beauty Parlor," "Appetizers," "Difficulties," with each of the over 1,600 up-to-date practical entries numbered, from 1, "yes," to 1,611, "the zipper," a tongue-twister *Say It in Yiddish* renders, in roman letters, as "BLITS-shleh-s'l." There were words and phrases to get the traveler through a visit to the post office to buy stamps in Yiddish, and through a visit to the doctor to take care of that "krahmpf" (1,317) after one has eaten too much of the "LEH-ber mit TSIB-eh-less" (620) served at the cheap "res-taw-RAHN" (495) just down the "EH-veh-new" (197) from one's "haw-TEL" (103).

One possible explanation of at least part of the absurd poignance of *Say It in Yiddish* presented itself: that its list of words and phrases was standard throughout the "Say It" series. Once one accepted the proposition of a modern Yiddish phrase book, Yiddish versions of such phrases as "Where can I get a social-security card?" and "Can you help me jack up the car?", taken in the context of the book's part of a uniform series, became more understandable.

But an examination of the specific examples chosen for inclusion under the various, presumably standard, rubrics revealed that the Weinreichs had indeed served as editors here, and considered their supposedly useful phrases with care, selecting, for example, to give Yiddish translations for the English names of the following foods, none of them very likely to be found under "Food" in the Swahili, Japanese, or Malay books in the series: stuffed cabbage, kreplach, blintzes, matzo, lox, corned beef, herring, kugel, tsimmis, and schav. The fact that most of these words did not seem to require much work to get them into Yiddish suggested that *Say It in Yiddish* had been edited with a particular kind of reader in mind, the reader who was traveling, or planned to travel, to a very particular kind of place, a place where one could expect to find both "ahn OON-tehr-bahn" (subway) and "geh-FIL-teh FISH."

I could neither understand nor stop considering, stop wondering and dreaming about, the intended nature and purpose of the book. Was the original 1958 Dover edition simply the reprint of some earlier, less heartbreakingly implausible book? At what time in the history of the world had there been a place of the kind that the Weinreichs' work implied, a place where not only the doctors and waiters and trolley conductors spoke Yiddish, but also the airline clerks, travel agents, ferry captains, and casino employees? A place where you could have rented a summer home from Yiddish speakers, gone to a Yiddish movie, gotten a finger wave from a Yiddish-speaking hairstylist, a shoeshine from a Yiddish-speaking shine boy, and then had your dental bridge repaired by a Yiddish-speaking dentist? If, as seemed likelier, the book first saw light in 1958, a full ten years after the founding of the country that turned its back once and for all on the Yiddish language, condemning it to watch the last of its native speakers die one by one in a headlong race for extinction with the twentieth century itself, then the tragic dimension of the joke loomed larger, and made the Weinreichs' intention even harder to divine. It seemed an entirely futile effort on the part of its authors, a gesture of embittered hope, of valedictory daydreaming, of a utopian impulse turned cruel and ironic.

Say It in Yiddish laid out, with numerical precision, the outlines of a world, of a fantastic land in which it would behoove you to know how to say, in Yiddish,

250. What is the flight number?

1,372. I need something for a tourniquet.

1,379. Here is my identification.

254. Can I go by boat/ferry to _____?

The blank in the last of those phrases, impossible to fill in, tantalized me. Whither could I sail on that boat/ferry, in the solicitous company of Uriel and Beatrice Weinreich, and from what shore?

I dreamed of at least two possible destinations. The first one was a modern independent state very closely analogous to the State of Israel—call it the State of Yisroel—a postwar Jewish homeland created during a time of moral emergency, located presumably, but not necessarily, in Palestine; it could have been in Alaska, or in Madagascar. Here, perhaps, that minority faction of the Zionist movement who favored the establishment of Yiddish as the national language of the Jews were able to prevail over its more numerous Hebraist opponents. There would be Yiddish color commentators for soccer games, Yiddish-speaking cash machines, Yiddish tags on the collars of dogs. Public debate, private discourse, joking and lamentation, all would be conducted not in a new-old, partly artificial language like Hebrew, a prefabricated skyscraper still under construction, with only the lowermost of its stories as yet inhabited by the generations, but in a tumbledown old palace capable in the smallest of its stones (the word "*nu*") of expressing slyness, tenderness, derision, romance, disputation, hopefulness, skepticism, sorrow, a lascivious impulse, or the confirmation of one's worst fears.

The implications of this change on the official language of the "Jewish homeland," a change which, depending on your view of human character and its underpinnings, was either minor or fundamental, were difficult to sort out. I couldn't help thinking that such a nation, speaking its essentially European tongue, would, in the Middle East, stick out among its neighbors to an even greater degree than Israel does now. But would the Jews of a Mediterranean Yisroel be impugned and admired for having the same kind of character that Israelis, rightly or wrongly, are widely taken to have, the classic sabra personality: rude, scrappy, loud, tough, secular, hardheaded, cagey, pushy? Was it living in a near-permanent state of war, or was it the Hebrew language, or something else, that had made Israeli humor so dark, so barbed, so cynical, so untranslatable? Perhaps this Yisroel, like its cognate in our own world, had the potential to seem a frightening, even a harrowing place, as the following sequence from the section on "Difficulties" seemed to imply:

109. What is the matter here?
110. What am I to do?
112. They are bothering me.
113. Go away.
114. I will call a policeman.

In an essay that I wrote and eventually published in *Civilization* magazine—and from which I am here liberally quoting—I tried to imagine one possible Yisroel: the youngest nation on the North American continent, founded in the former Alaska Territory during World War II as a resettlement zone for the Jews of Europe. (For a brief while, I had once read, the Roosevelt administration had proposed such a plan.) The resulting country would be a far different place than Israel. It would be a cold, northern land of furs, paprika, samovars, and one long, glorious day of summer. It would be absurd to speak Hebrew, that tongue of spikenard and almonds, in such a place. This Yisroel—or maybe it would be called Alyeska—I imagined at the time as a kind of Jewish Sweden, social-democratic, resource rich, prosperous, organizationally and temperamentally far more akin to its immediate neighbor, Canada, than to its more freewheeling benefactor far to the south. Perhaps, indeed, there might have been some conflict, in the years since independence, between the United States and Alyeska.

This country I thought of was in the nature of a wistful fantasyland, a toy theater with miniature sets and furnishings to arrange and rearrange, painted backdrops on which the gleaming lineaments of a snowy Jewish Onhava could be glimpsed, all its grief concealed behind the scrim, hidden in the machinery of the loft, sealed up beneath trapdoors in the floorboards. But there was another destination to which the Weinreichs beckoned, unwittingly but in all the detail that Dover's "Say It" series required: home, to the "old country." To Europe.

In this Europe the millions of Jews who were never killed would have produced grandchildren, and great-grandchildren, and great-great-grandchildren. The countryside would retain large pockets of country people whose first language was still Yiddish, and in the cities one could find many more for whom Yiddish would be the language of kitchen and family, of theater and poetry and scholarship. A surprisingly large number of these people would be my relations. I would be able to go visit them, the way Irish Americans I knew were always visiting second and third cousins in Galway or Cork, sleeping in their strange beds, eating their strange food, and looking just like them. Imagine. Perhaps one of my cousins might take me to visit the house where my father's mother was born, or to the school in Vilna that my grandfather's grandfather attended with the boy Abraham Cahan. For my relatives, though they would doubtless know at least some English, I would want to trot out a few appropriate Yiddish phrases, more than anything as a way of reestablishing the tenuous connection between us; in this world Yiddish would not be, as it is in ours, a tin can with no tin can on the other end of the string. Here, though

I would be able to get by without them, I would be glad to have the Weinreichs along. Who knows but that visting some remote Polish backwater I might be compelled to visit a dentist to whom I would want to cry out, having found the appropriate number (1,447), "eer TOOT meer VAY!"

What would this Europe be like, I wondered, with its 25, 30, or 35 million Jews? Would they be tolerated, despised, ignored by, or merely indistinguishable from their fellow modern Europeans? What would the world be like, never having felt the need to create an Israel, that hard bit of grit in the socket that hinges Africa to Asia?

What, I wondered in the conclusion of my original essay, did it mean to originate from a place, from a world, from a culture that no longer existed, from a language that might die in my generation? What phrases would I need to know in order to speak to those millions of unborn phantoms to whom I belonged?

Just what was I supposed to do with this book?

5.

Not long after the essay on *Say It in Yiddish* was published in *Civilization*, I received a puckish email from my uncle Stan— the late Stanley Werbow, my grandmother's brother, a noted scholar of German and an American-born native speaker of Yiddish—congratulating me on having accomplished the trick, never especially difficult, of outraging Yiddishists.

The offended parties belonged to an Internet listserv called Mendele, which provides an electronic forum for a freewheeling discussion—its tone ranging from academic to informal, from humorous to dry as dust—of Yiddish and Yiddish culture, and to which my uncle Stan was himself a subscriber.

The Yiddish language evolved over the course of the thousand years following the migration of Jews into Western Europe and up to 1939, at which date its literature ranked among the glories of world heritage. About half of its approximately 11 million speakers were murdered during the Holocaust, with the rest dispersed, assimilated into other languages, or passed on, without passing on Yiddish. It continues to be spoken today as a home language by a far smaller if indeterminate number of older people and ultraorthodox Jews, and as a second language by scholars, students, and those devotees, like many of the subscribers to Mendele, who have made learning and preserving it their passionate pastime.

It turned out, when I took Uncle Stan up on his tip, that some of the Mendelyaners, as the listserv's members style themselves, were angry because of my essay, to which they had first been alerted by the following post:

Date: Mon, 23 Jun 1997
Subject: Weinreich's phrase book

I should like to alert the readers of this list to a delightfully humorous essay regarding Uriel and Beatrice Weinreich's little paperback phrase book *Say It in Yiddish* in the current (June–July 1997) issue of *Civilization* [The Magazine of The Library of Congress]. The essay is entitled "Guidebook to a Land of Ghosts" and is subtitled "A Yiddish phrase book is an absurd, poignant artifact of a country that never was." The writer, Michael Chabon, finds, in the pages of the phrase book, detailed directions—buying plane tickets, visiting the dentist, getting a finger wave from a Yiddish-speaking hairdresser or a shoeshine from a Yiddish-speaking shineboy—in a country that never existed. The charming illustrations by Ben Katchor...

This initial post was followed two days later by:

Date: Wed, 25 Jun 1997
Subject: Weinreich's phrase book

I have to take issue with the note... regarding an article in the magazine *Civilization* about the above book. I haven't read the article (nor do I intend to, based on [the previous] review), but I find reference to Ashkenaz as "a country that never was" quite offensive and not "delightfully humorous" at all... The author of this piece should be excoriated rather than praised for this article, and placed in the same kheyrem as the rest of those who think Yiddish is dead.

To be *excoriated*, by the way, literally means "to have one's skin removed"; it's the heavy-duty version of *exfoliated*. Soon afterward, another angry Yiddishist came after me brandishing his loofa of outrage:

Listen up friend Chabon.* A number of us have gotten together and created a dictionary of chemistry, in Yiddish!! (I hope it will come out in a short time)... And who needs it...?? WE need it because it is our Yiddish

---

* This post is a literal translation, by its author, of the Yiddish original; in Yiddish the word *chaver* (lit., "friend"), when used as a form of address, has a number of possible shades of meaning, among them, as here, "enemy," or "dickhead."

> CULTURE... for the same reason the Guide for Travelers
> is needed... throughout the world...

The whole *tsimmes* went on more or less in this fashion, with some Mendelanyers writing to defend what I had written, and with the argument on the other side boiling down in the end mostly to this:

> Of course, no one can fault him for how he feels about the issue, but it seems to me that this feeling stems at least in part from his sharing the popular but quite inaccurate opinion that Yiddish has already entered the world of Latin, Sanskrit, and Gothic.

Of course, this misses the point completely. It is not the apparent "deadness" of its language, however accurate or inaccurate such an impression may be, that makes *Say It in Yiddish* such a wondrous, provocative, sad, and funny book. Even if Yiddish is taken to be alive and well, *Say It in Yiddish* still proposes a world that never was and might have been, and makes it all feel absurdly and beautifully ordinary. But though I wrote to the membership and tried to explain myself, I had no success in diminishing the rage of Mendelyaners such as the one who declared, finally:

> The "humorous" article in *Civilization* was not funny, but ridiculous. No, an ignorant insult to the World of Yiddish. The author of that article has already apologized to B. Weinreich.

In fact I had, after the article was published, received a very unhappy letter from Mrs. Weinreich, the widow of Uriel, who died in 1967. She viewed my essay as disrespectful and mocking not only of her late husband, who as I now learned had at his untimely death been regarded as the great young hope of Yiddish scholarship in America, but of the Yiddish language itself. And so I *had* written her to apologize, not for anything I said in the essay, but for any unintended appearance of mockery there might have been, and for having hurt her feelings. To this I received a not-at-all mollified reply to my reply.

Back in 1991, the reviewer of my first story collection in the *New York Times Book Review* criticized me for being, among a number of other things, essentially too much of a nice Jewish boy. Too polite, she lamented. Too respectful of my elders. "Mr. Chabon's parents," said the reviewer, Elizabeth Benedict, "may not appreciate my holding up Philip Roth as an example to their son, but Mr. Roth offers crucial lessons to this... young writer, who is so evidently eager to please... Don't worry so much about being nice." I supposed, at the time, that the *Times* reviewer had a point; and since then, I have encountered nothing that would persuade me otherwise, or that would enable me, however hard I might try, to be anything else. And as a nice Jewish boy, I experienced two competing reactions to this *tsimmes* over *Say It in Yiddish*, both of them typical if not definitive, to my mind, of my lamentable species.

On the one hand, I was, as I wrote to Mrs. Weinreich, deeply sorry. I had never been in hot water before because of something I wrote, and I found that I did not enjoy the sensation. As Elizabeth Benedict suggested, I wanted people to like me. And over and above every other kind of people whom I wanted to like me were nice old Jewish ladies like Beatrice Weinreich. Even stronger than my regret was my sense of embarrassment. Many of my Mendele critics had taken the time to "hock me a *tchainik*" about my ignorance of Yiddish and Yiddishkeit, and while I freely confessed to this ignorance, it is one thing to admit something and another to have it thrown in your face. The embarrassing fact was that I had never *heard* of Uriel Weinreich, and the reverence in which he was evidently held persuaded me that I ought to have. I *felt* my ignorance, and was ashamed.

My second typical nice-Jewish-boy reaction was—well, I'll get to that in a minute.

Some time after the tsimmes cooled, Janet Hadda, a professor of Yiddish lit at UCLA and a practicing psychoanalyst, wrote a series of articles and papers in which she tried to determine just what it was about my essay that had made some people so angry. Hadda claimed that the lovers of Yiddish were in mourning over their murdered language, and hence living in denial, a stage from which, as we all know, it is but one short step to anger. There may or may not be merit to Hadda's argument; I would prefer to leave it to the analysts and analysands to duke it out for themselves, if they care to. I was more taken by another of Hadda's claims, namely her postulating beyond questions of death and denial a kind of survival of Yiddishkeit in the imagination of my generation of American Jewish writers, in our return to Ashkenazic and Yiddish themes and subject matter, in our evocation, perhaps half-unconscious, of the deep echoes of the mother tongue of our grandparents and great-grandparents. Hadda describes us as "born into an interrupted culture" and "try[ing] to compensate for the loss."

> The phenomenon of young writers turning to the cul-
> ture of their parents for exploration is anything but rare.
> What is unusual, if not unique, about the culture of Ash-

kenaz † is that it can no longer be found today except in
the memories of a very few survivors and *in the imaginations of artists* [italics mine].

Another phenomenon that is far from rare, of course, is that
of a Jew—hell, of any human being—longing for a home that
feels irretrievable yet never ceases, age after age, to beckon.
Perhaps one explanation for the improbably long survival of
Judaism is the fitness of one of its central images—the unending
loss of Jerusalem—to our innate human talent for nostalgia, to
the aetataureate delusion, our false but certain collective human
memory of a Golden Age, a time when doors had no locks and
a man's word was his bond and giants walked the earth. You
find an expression of the same sense of irrecoverable loss in
the "Intimations of Immortality," where the part of Jerusalem
is played by Childhood, a structure that in Wordsworthian
retrospect appears to have been built, like the Golden City,
nearer somehow to the heart of the mystery of things. And this
is where, for me, genre fiction comes into the picture. Because
when you are talking, like Hadda, about lands that can be found
only in the imagination, you are really speaking my language—
my *mamaloshen*.

6.

I was born the first time in Georgetown University Hospital,
in 1963, and the second time ten years later, in the opening
pages of "A Scandal in Bohemia." In this latter infancy the

---

† By Ashkenaz, Hadda means an actual geographical region—the lands of northern
European Jewry—as much as a culture and a state of mind.

heaven that lay about *me* was the work of Conan Doyle, Ray Bradbury, Philip José Farmer, Jack Vance. Fantasy and science fiction, then horror and hard-boiled mystery; my passion and my ambition as a reader and a writer were forged in the smithy of genre fiction.

As a young man, an English major, and a regular participant in undergraduate fiction-writing workshops, I was taught—or perhaps in fairness it would be more accurate to say I learned— that science fiction was not serious fiction, that a writer of mystery novels might be loved but not revered, that if I meant to get serious about the art of fiction I might set a novel in Pittsburgh but never on Pluto. *The Long Goodbye* could be parsed by the literary critic for a class on Masculine Anxiety in the Postwar American Novel, but it was unlikely to appear on the syllabus of a general twentieth-century American literature class alongside *Absalom, Absalom* and the stories of Flannery O'Connor.

There were exceptions, writers whose work drew overtly on sources in genre fiction and yet was taken seriously by critics, scholars, and general readers. They had names like Pynchon, Burroughs, Vonnegut, Nabokov, and their writing was often described as "transgressive," as if choosing a detective hero or an interplanetary setting were not merely ill-advised if you hoped to make literature but violated an outright taboo. A detective novelist or a horror writer who made claims to artistry sat in the same chair at the table of literature as did a transvestite cousin at a family Thanksgiving. He was something to be allowed for, indulged, pardoned, excused, his fabulous hat studiously ignored.

I was twenty (let's say). I accepted this curious ethos as indisputable, and found a strong appeal in the idea of transgression. I wrote a raft of stories that cross-dressed in the clothes of genre and found sure enough that when I gave them out to workshops, workshops tended to look away from the ostrich feather in my hat. "I don't know anything about mysteries," said the reader of one of my short stories, a surrealist effort featuring a gumshoe working a puzzling murder in a De Chirico city, written under the heavy influence of Chandler and Donald Barthelme. "I hate science fiction," went another frequently offered bit of helpful criticism, "so there's nothing I can really do to help you with this."

When I first visited the campus of UC Irvine, where I eventually enrolled in the MFA writing program, I was ushered, with the kind of clueless goodwill that might impel you to introduce the only two Mennonites at your wedding to each other, into the company of Gregory Benford, a fine writer of extremely "hard" science fiction (*Timescape, Across the Sea of Suns*) and a professor in the UCI Department of Physics and Astronomy. I don't remember now if Professor Benford had read any of my undergraduate work, or was only going on my description of it, but I do remember his polite and kindly bafflement.

A lonely business, transgressing. There was nothing that anybody could do for me. I laid aside the epic novel I had been planning, about a Holmesian detective investigating, on Earth and along the canals of the planet Mars, the disappearance of the great and greatly mistaken astronomer Percival Lowell, and turned instead to concentrate on this other book, a straightforward realistic narrative, equally influenced by Proust, Fitzgerald, and Philip Roth, about summertime and sexual identity in the city of Pittsburgh.

It was in this period, when I abandoned the career that was both to have culminated in and been launched by that novel about Mars, that I also turned my back on Judaism. I was learning to question everything; I guess I was trying to fit in.

Nothing about my being Jewish—about my ancestors, about their languages and histories, about the stale holiday invocations of freedom, continuity, and survival—seemed to have use or relation to the ongoing business of my life at the time. Israel had lost its heroic claim on my imagination and seemed to have become, by means I did not understand, the ally and stooge of a Disneyfied president I loathed. In the meantime my mother moved away from the town where I grew up. I married a woman who was not Jewish, and began work on what was to be my second novel. I had no home, and neither, it seemed to me, did anyone—remember that I was living, at the time, in Southern California.

For a while, still young and interested in my own pain as an object of the world's attention, I grooved along on my lostness. But after a while I got tired of feeling that way. That first marriage broke up, and the novel that was to be my second was even more doomed than the marriage. I wanted to know where I came from, to retrace my steps and see if I dropped anything along the way that might serve me, now, better than I had imagined at the time of letting it go.

I started to light candles; I met and married my present wife, the grandchild of European Jewish immigrants; I abandoned the novel and began the long wandering back to a place where I could feel at home.

I kept thinking about those Jews up there in Alaska, making their Yiddishland. And I kept thinking about genre and about the books I had always thought I was going to write. And little by little at first, and then all at once, the idea began to assemble itself: I would build myself a home in my imagination as my wife and I were making a home in the world. That idea led to the writing of my novel *The Yiddish Policemen's Union*, set, with a kind of rapturous apprehension, in a place where the Weinreichs' phrase book would come in very handy indeed.

It was as I made the laborious and thrilling move from reverie to fiction that I found myself driven by the second key element, to which I alluded earlier, of being a nice Jewish boy. Because if you are a nice Jewish boy, as Rav Philip Roth has conclusively proven, you are also, on some level, a *mazik*: there's a devil in you, driving you to say, and to do, and to write things that you know you must or ought not say, do, or write. Like my uncle Stan with his mischievous email, the nice Jewish boy lives in thrall, at least some of the time, to the spirit of doing things *af tselokhis*, out of spite, a kind of magical, Trickster spite that, like Coyote or Loki of the Northmen, is responsible for all destruction and all creation too.

If I could outrage a few people with one little essay—how many could I piss off with an entire *novel*?

GOLEMS I HAVE KNOWN,
OR, WHY MY ELDER SON'S
MIDDLE NAME IS NAPOLEON

A Trickster's Memoir

I SAW MY FIRST golem in 1968, in Flushing, New York, shortly before my fifth birthday. It lay on a workbench in the basement of my uncle Jack's house, a few blocks away from the duplex—we called it a "two-family house"—that my parents and I shared with a Greek couple, who lived upstairs. My uncle Jack owned a candy store in Harlem, in a neighborhood where there had once been only Jews but now there were only black people, though my uncle Jack did not call them that. He called them "the coloreds." Nevertheless he always hired local Harlem people to work in his store, and he extended credit to many families in the neighborhood. I suppose he had complicated feelings about his customers, and they about him, both as a creditor and as a cranky and ill-humored man. Owning a candy store was not my uncle Jack's choice of employment; he had failed at several other trades before finally arriving, with the last of his and my aunt's savings, at the threshold of Mount Morris Candy and News. Though I was not told and did not understand any of this until much later, Uncle Jack was also a devoted Jewish scholar who nightly studied Torah and Talmud, and who had in the past year or so embarked upon the study of kabbalah, that body of Jewish mystical teachings that have produced the Zohar, the false messiah Sabbatai Zevi, and a sense of deep understanding and inner peace, or so one presumes, for Madonna and Roseanne Barr. My parents and my uncle and aunt were not especially close, but we lived so near to them that inevitably we ended up spending time at their house, and I soon learned to fear and to long to see whatever was going on down there in Uncle Jack's basement, to which he invariably repaired as soon as decency and the serving of the babka allowed.

This all happened so long ago, and I was, it will be recalled, so young at the time that it's hard for me to remember just how I contrived to convey myself down there under the house, into the basement, which I had been told in no uncertain terms was filled with all kinds of deliciously dangerous power tools and chemicals, and hence strictly off-limits, to have a look. If I were writing a short story, I would figure out how to get the parents out of the way, start them arguing bitterly about Vietnam or civil rights at the dinner table, and then have my fictionalized self slip away unnoticed, perhaps with a vague murmur about going to look at the money plants in the backyard, to head down the long dark stairway into the basement, with its smell of iron filings and cold linoleum. Since this is a memoir, though, I will be truthful and say I don't know how I managed the trick. But I remember the dark stairs, and the cold iron smell.

I'm sure you will doubt what I tell you next, putting it down to the flawed memory of a small boy with a big imagination, or perhaps even, considering what I am about to say, thinking it all nothing but a pack of lies. That's precisely why I've never said anything about the real golems in my life before now. There was a golem—the most famous golem of all, the Golem of Prague— in my novel *The Amazing Adventures of Kavalier & Clay*, and since it was published a lot of people have asked me about my interest in that golem and in golems in general. And, because I was afraid to tell the truth and more interested in sounding smart than in sounding crazy, I usually said something about having seen, as a child, a still image from Paul Wegener's 1915 film *Der Golem* in a book about fantastic cinema, as if that explained anything, and then after that I would often say something sort of profound and sententious about how the relationship between a golem and its creator is usually viewed as a metaphor for that between the work of art—in my case, a novel—and its creator, and how my ideas about golems had been shaped by reading Gershom Scholem's famous essay "On the Idea of the Golem," and blah, blah, blah. When the truth is that golems are real, they are out there now, and they are everywhere. Well, not everywhere, perhaps, but I've seen a bunch of them in my own lifetime, and that's without even trying—believe you me—to find them. As for the Golem of Prague, and the thinly fictionalized role it plays both in *Kavalier & Clay* and in my life, I'm going to come to that in time.

I'm aware, in making this confession, that I'm revealing something that some of you already know perfectly well, something that is generally agreed to be better left undiscussed. I don't think it's exactly taboo for me to reveal the truth about golems—God, I hope not—but what do I know? I've never studied kabbalah. If you see shadowy people follow me out of the hall tonight, or if a blow dart suddenly appears in my larynx and I keel over midsentence, you will know that I must have transgressed. I don't know what exactly is prompting me to come forward now and come out with the truth. I think it has something to do with turning forty, with the growing desire I feel to look backward over my life and to try to shore together, if I can, some kind of retrospective understanding, some sense of meaning and perhaps even wisdom to impart to my children as they grow into full consciousness of the pain and mystery of life. Maybe it has something to do with having won the Pulitzer Prize, which gives a guy a sense, however mistaken, of authority, and which, as far as I know, they will not take away from you even if it is determined that you have lost your mind.

In any event, what I saw when I reached the inner sanctum of Uncle Jack's workshop, with its tools hanging neatly from their hooks, its table saw and drill press, its swept pile of sawdust in the corner, tidily awaiting the dustpan, was a golem. For those of you who may not, still, be aware of or understand just what exactly a golem is, let me briefly state that a golem is an artificial being, usually but not necessarily human in shape, made from a lump of clay or earth—the word "golem" comes from an ancient Hebrew word meaning "lump"—and brought to life, or to a semblance of life, by mystical means. Some golems are animated by the placing under their tongues of a tablet with one of the names of God written on it, others by having the Hebrew word *emet*, "truth," graved onto their broad foreheads, still others by some combination of the two. But in common all golems require above all that a complicated series of alphabetical spells be chanted over them, in the proper order and combination, for hours and hours and hours. Now, according to the great Herr Scholem, the point of golem-making has been greatly exaggerated over the years, embroidered by liars and legend-tellers and romancers. Originally one—and when I say "one" I mean "a trained adept acting in concert with at least one other trained adept"—originally one made a golem not in the hope of bringing it to life but in the hope of bringing oneself to life. It was a kind of meditative exercise designed, like other kinds of chanting rituals, to free the consciousness. One imitated God's creation of Adam in the hope of approaching knowledge of the ecstasy and power of that creation.

At any rate, looking back on it, I don't seriously think my uncle Jack could have had any sincere expectation of bringing his own golem, the Golem of Flushing, to life. I am certain that it was intended only as a vehicle for expanding his consciousness of the Ineffable Name. It lay, as I have said, on his workbench, a big pine slab which he had nailed together himself years before. Honestly I don't remember all that much about how his golem looked; it had big feet, each with five clay toes; its head was squarish, its nose flat, its hair scratched in with some pointed tool in wiggly swirls. I remember the color of its skin, or rather of the clay from which it had been formed, hardened curds or handfuls of clay that were a rich dark brown like coffee grounds. A colored, I thought. The thing that impressed me the most about the thing was the air of utter inertness that it gave off, something more than lifelessness, heavier and more oppressive. In later years I would think of this golem when I saw cigar-store Indians, and again when I saw the giant lumpy head of John F. Kennedy in the lobby of the Kennedy Center in Washington, D.C. Its eyes were a pair of horizontal slits, slightly bulging, meant to suggest, I suppose, that it was sleeping.

What did I make of it, at the time? I knew, of course, that it was not a real person—Uncle Jack was clearly not the most talented sculptor in the world—but there was something about it that troubled me; it had presence. I wasn't quite afraid of it, or rather I feared it obscurely, and with a stab of bright curiosity, as I feared and wondered about all kinds of other elements of the world of adults—my mother's pressing ham, filled with mysterious sand; the heavy wooden trays in which my father kept his microscope slides, smeared with the lung tissue of monkeys. There seemed inherent in that dark clay doll on the table a purpose and a power beyond my imagining.

What can I say? I reached out to touch it, grabbing clumsily at the thing's left big toe, and the toe came off with a dry tinkling of dust. That was the kind of kid I was. I had poked a hole in my mother's pressing ham so that forever after it leaked sand; I had broken five or six of my father's pneumococcus slides. And in my horror at this act of accidental mutilation—and I'm perfectly willing to admit that it was only this, the action of horror and dismay on a childish imagination—I saw the Golem of Flushing open its eyes. I will never forget the sight of the dull, wet gaze, blank, ignorant, afraid, that lighted on my face at that instant. I have no idea how I managed to get out of the basement again. The next thing I remember is sitting in my aunt's living room, on the slick crinkling plastic of her slipcovered sofa, and hearing my uncle Jack cry out, his voice ragged and cracked, "They killed King!" "Oh, no," I heard my mother say. "Oh, that's just awful." "King who?" I asked, thinking that they were lamenting the death of some monarch.

The night I broke a toe off the Golem of Flushing was the night, as it turned out—April 4, 1968—on which James Earl Ray shot Martin Luther King Jr. There was some rioting over in Harlem, in the course of which somebody set fire to the block that comprised Mount Morris Candy and News, and Uncle Jack's last-chance enterprise was burned out. In the jumble of misunderstood and half-interpreted news reports, anxious talk, and curt whispering that surrounded this calamity and that seemed to make up the bulk of adult conversation in the week that followed, I heard repeated references to "the black man." Inevitably, I guess, I was forced to the conclusion that it had been the dark man of clay in Uncle Jack's basement, angered perhaps by the loss of his toe, who had gone out to Harlem and burnt down the candy store. And it was all my fault.

I was beginning to learn the bitter truth about golems. A golem, like a lie, is the expression of a wish: a wish for peace and security; a wish for strength and control; a wish to know, in a tiny, human way, a thousandth of a millionth of the joy and power of the Greater Creation. And nothing I have learned since has ever been able to dissuade me that on that April night a golem, charged with all the wishes, dark and light, of a suffering people, was created and set loose in the world.

Soon after his world was set on fire, my uncle Jack fell while chasing after a young black neighborhood kid who had, or so he imagined, called him "Hymie." He broke his hip. He went into a rapid decline after that, and was dead before the following autumn. It was around that time that I managed to get down into the basement again. This part may be the embroidery of a guilty recollection, but I remember it as being on the actual day of Jack's funeral, when we all went back to the house to start the weeklong period of shivah. As I had suspected it would be, the giant doll with the dead, fearful eyes was gone. I got down on my hands and knees and looked around, and there, under the now barren workbench, lay the toe.

After a while my father came downstairs looking for me. Since he didn't seem to be angry at finding me in such close proximity to dangerous tools and chemicals, not to mention trespassing into forbidden zones of mystic knowledge, I told him the whole story. He laughed, and reassured me that I was not in any way responsible for my uncle's death, explaining that Uncle Jack had had his little

0.5

eccentricities when it came to religion. But I could see that my father was not taking me seriously. So I showed him the toe.

"Well," he said, studying it, taking me a little more seriously now, it seemed to me. "If you had brought it to life, that wouldn't be too surprising, I guess. You know, Michael, we're descended on my father's side from Rabbi Judah ben Loew."

It was then and there, and not from any book on fantastic cinema, that I first learned about golems and in particular the Golem of Prague. My father explained to me that it was the great Rabbi Judah of Prague who, sometime in the sixteenth century, created the best-known of all golems to do his bidding around the synagogue, sweeping up the dooryard and readying the sanctuary for the Sabbath, and to help protect the Jews of Prague's ghetto against those who sought to harm them. This golem, like a lie, grew to a tremendous size, and in its vengeful might came in time to threaten the security of those it had been made to keep safe. Rabbi Judah lost control of it, and eventually he was obliged to destroy the life he had talked into being, in order to keep it from destroying everything else. And it was from this great wonder-working rabbi, through a grandson who left Prague and traveled across the Austrian Empire to settle in Lodz, that we were descended. Or so my father said. He had told me such things before, about other famous Jews from history, and he would continue, as I grew older, to periodically reveal new and ever more startling connections.

A writer of science fiction named Philip José Farmer once devised the amusing or tedious conceit of tracing the lineage of Lord Greystoke, better known as Tarzan of the Apes. Mr. Farmer postulated that an ancestor of the future lord of the jungle was among the passengers of two coaches that were passing Wold Newton, England, in 1795, just as a radioactive meteor fell from outer space into a meadow on the outskirts of the village. The radiation from the space rock, and the genetic mutation it caused, Mr. Farmer posited, affected all the descendents of those passengers, among them the eventual John Clayton, Lord Greystoke—Tarzan. Mr. Farmer then extended his conceit by claiming that not only Tarzan but all the great heroes and villains of popular nineteenth- and twentieth-century literature—the Scarlet Pimpernel, Sherlock Holmes and Professor Moriarty, Doc Savage, Phileas Fogg, Fu Manchu, Sam Spade, James Bond—were descended from the people riding in that pair of coaches, a superhuman lineage of siblings and cousins descended from that common ancestor and that catastrophic event.

When, as a boy of nine or ten, I encountered Mr. Farmer's hypothesis in his amusing mock biography of Tarzan, it came as no surprise to me at all. My father had already articulated, in considerable detail, a similar startling theory of our own lineage.

Over the years my father has informed me—generally with no warning and without offering any explanation for the information's having gone unmentioned until that moment— that we Chabons are connected, distantly perhaps but with a kind of telling intimacy, to the following people: the great *tragedienne* Rachel, the humorist Art Buchwald, the vicious murderer Lepke Buchalter, Rabbi Eliyahu, known as the Gaon or Genius of Vilna, the aforementioned Rabbi Judah ben Bezalel ben Loew, Harry Houdini, the first-class spy and third-rate baseball player Moe Berg, and, most gloriously of all, Napoleon Bonaparte, through his nephew Napoleon III, who—or so my father claims—fathered an illegimate child, my ancestor, of the above-mentioned French actress, Rachel.

I won't bother with the question of whether my father is telling the truth, or believes he is telling the truth, when he says such things. Nor is it germane to my point to ask if I believe him. After all, what he says could be true; if plausibility is good enough for me as a reader, and good enough for you as listeners, it's good enough for me as a son. The importance to me, now and as a child, of my father's stories is and was 1) their peculiar, detailed beauty, from the quirkiness of the famous personalities they involved to the complicated ways in which my father attempted to map out our relation to these people, and 2) the sense of incredible connectedness I derived, as a kid, from his stories. Listening to my father describe the deeds, crimes, and achievements of our famous cousins, scattered as they were across continents and eras, gave me an almost vertiginous sense of simultaneity, of our family's and my own small self's existing in all times, at all places.

When I was ten years old—shortly after reading Philip José Farmer's biography of Tarzan, with its genealogy of heroes and criminals almost as fantastic as my own—I produced my first sustained work of fiction. This was a short story, about twelve pages in length, entitled "The Revenge of Captain Nemo." It recounted a meeting between Verne's Captain Nemo and Doyle's Sherlock Holmes (first cousins, according to Farmer). I won't make any claims as to its merits, but two great things happened to me in the course of writing it. One was that I consciously adopted, for the first time, a literary style: Sir Arthur Conan Doyle's, or rather that of the good Dr. John Watson. I think I had always been sensitive, before this, to variations in writers' diction and to the mood and tone of a paragraph. I was alert to the difference in vocabulary and idiom one found in British storybooks, could tell when language was trying to sound antiquated, jocular, or hard-boiled. I could hear the difference between words of Latin origin and those that came from Anglo-Saxon. I knew how Doyle's writing sounded. I could hear the tune of it in my head. Now I just had to sit down and play.

Getting the style down—that was more than half the fun for me. I used words like "postulated" and "retribution." I wrote "had the odor of" instead of "smelled." I went on about railway schedules, the harbor at Portsmouth, the fog. I referred to the infamous Moriarty as "the Napoleon of Crime," thus linking him, in my imagination, to my own family tree. When I finished it, "The Revenge of Captain Nemo" went over pretty well. I had the satisfaction of being praised by my parents and other adults and of having actually completed something that struck me as admirably substantial, even huge. The work of typing it alone had nearly killed me. But more precious to me than praise or completion was the intense pleasure I had derived from attempting to impersonate Sir Arthur Conan Doyle, from putting on his accent, following his verbal trail. It was the pleasure that a liar takes in his lie as it enters the world wearing the accent and raiment of the truth, sounding so right and plausible that—if he is any kind of liar at all—he begins, himself, to believe it. It was the pleasure that a maker of golems takes as the force of his words, the rhythm and accuracy of his alphabetical spells, blow life into the cold clay nostrils, and the great stony hand unclenches and reaches for his own. At some point in the exercise the power of Doyle's diction resounding in my ear carried me away. I felt intimately connected to him, as though it was not I inhabiting his literary skin but, somehow, the other way around. It was like something out of a ghost story—a child sitting down at a haunted piano and feeling a spectral hand guide his own over the keys.

That was the second important thing that happened to me when I wrote that story. It was as if I had opened a door and stepped into the room in which all my favorite writers were sitting around waiting for me to show up. They were a disparate bunch, from Judy Blume to Edgar Allan Poe, spread over different eras, continents, and genres. Some were close kin to each other—Lord Dunsany, H. P. Lovecraft—while others seemed to have nothing in common beyond their connection to me. And somehow, I sensed, their intersection defined me. They were, in other words, my family. I derived from them, they explained me. And more than anything else I wanted—I knew it now—to be accounted one of them. This was the wish—to be a credit to that far-flung family of literary heroes—that I have sought to embody, to express in the infinitely malleable clay of language, ever since.

It was around this time, as I was making up my mind to be a writer, that I encountered my second golem. By this time we were living in the then-new town of Columbia, a planned community in the Maryland suburbs, between Baltimore and Washington, D.C. In the waning years of my parents' marriage—it ended, draw your own conclusions, the year that I began to formulate my wish—one of the only reliable sources of pleasure for my father and me was the weekly trip we took, alone, to the Howard County Public Library's main branch, then located on Frederick Road, outside of the city limits of Columbia itself. One evening as I was rather sullenly spinning the wire rack of paperbacks intended for a group of readers who were then just becoming known, in the librarian trade, as YAs, I came across a book called *Strangely Enough!*, written by one C. B. Colby and published by Scholastic Book Services. It was one of those mysterious books that you have loved as a child but which as you go out into the world no one else ever seems to have read or even heard of, although the library's copy was tattered and well worn and had been checked out, to judge from the number of fading purplish dates stamped

onto its tan pocket, by dozens of YAs before me. It was made up
of a series of about a hundred short pieces, little essays, each about
five hundred words long and devoted to exposing or musing
over all kinds of inexplicable and supposedly factual incidents
and phenomena: poltergeists, haunted paintings, UFO sightings,
rains of frogs and stones, witch scares, phantom hitchhikers,
encounters with the devil in which he left his cloven footprint
clearly visible in a neighborhood rock. I read a few of the entries—
enough to persuade me that it was going to turn out to be one of
the best books I had ever read—and then carried it with a few
other titles to wait for my father at the circulation desk.

"*Strangely Enough!*" the librarian intoned, putting a little
Twilight Zone wobble into her voice. I nodded. "You know he lives
here. C. B. Colby."

It turned out that C. B. Colby lived not merely in Columbia
but right down the street from my family, in the small cubistic
house stained dark blue, with the goldfish pond, that you had
to pass whenever you went to our street's communal mailbox.
His real name was Joseph Adler, and in time I discovered
that in addition to *Strangely Enough!* he was the author of
some 250 other works, fiction and nonfiction, for children
and YAs, under a bewildering variety of pseudonyms. All
I had known of him before now was that he was a baby chick of
a man, with a soft, wavering plume of white hair and a gentle if
somewhat stiff manner toward children. A reticent, courtly ghost
of him, the first real writer I ever knew, can be glimpsed in the
figment of a writer called August Van Zorn, in my novel *Wonder
Boys*. Mrs. Adler had died not long after we moved into the
neighborhood, and my mother had made him a roast and carried
it down to him. The widower, she told me when she returned
from this charitable visit, was a "survivor." I hadn't heard the

term before, though I had an aunt by marriage who had been interned at Auschwitz as a child, and I knew enough, the next time I saw Mr. Adler, to look for and discover the greenish-black numbers on the inside of his forearm.

I was not a bold child. It took me most of the four-week circulation period to get up the nerve to go to his front door, clutching the library's copy of his book, which by now I had read at least half a dozen times, terrifying myself, ruining my sleep, making the flat, sunny, avocado-and-goldenrod-colored 1973 world of Columbia, Maryland into a strange and marvelous world that contained treasures and ghosts and mysterious bright objects in the sky. Before approaching his house directly, however, I had spent several days furtively lurking nearby, concealing myself behind a bush or the neighbor's parked car, studying the bare windows behind which nothing ever seemed to move. I saw a piano. I saw a work of iron sculpture that looked something like a mace and something like a gate and something like a twist of barbed wire. I saw thousand and thousands of books. And once I caught a glimpse of Mr. Adler, drinking orange juice straight from the carton.

"Ah," he said, when he opened the door to me. "My little shadow."

It would be nice to tell you a story now about how Mr. Adler, the taciturn, intellectual, widowed author of two hundred popular pseudonymous novels, and Michael Chabon, the awkward, unhappy, budding boy-writer skulking around the margins of his neighborhood, his future, and his parents' divorce, forged an unlikely friendship while teaching each other valuable lessons about literature and life. But it didn't work out that way; I guess that's why stories are so much better than life, or rather why stories make life so much better. Mr. Adler invited me in, dismissed *Strangely Enough!* with a contemptuous wave of his hand, poured me a glass of orange juice that I felt a little bit nervous about drinking, and told me that my eyeglasses were much too big for my face. The house was filled with all kinds of spiky and unnerving sculptures, some all welded steel, like the one I'd seen from the window, others done in wood, plaster, and glass. They were the work, he explained to me, of his wife. Just before I departed his house for the first and last time, he took me into his office and pointed to the neatly stacked pages of a manuscript sitting beside his great steely battleship of an IBM Selectric. "That is the first book I will ever put my own name upon," he said. There was a faint trace of an accent; it made me think of my aunt Renee, who had been in the camps too. "What kind of book is it?" I asked him. He looked annoyed. "It's a memoir, of course," he said. "The story of my life."

It was as he was walking me, almost herding me, really, toward the door, that I noticed, lying on the glass shelf of a chrome-plated étagère, what I took to be another example of his late wife's work. It was a clay doll, about the size of the old G.I. Joes they used to have—big enough to whip Ken's vinyl ass. This clay figure was lumpy and crooked and almost looked as if it had been made by a kid, and I remember considering whether I ought and then deciding not to ask Mr. Adler if he had any children. You could tell, somehow, that he did not. It was a just a glimpse that I got, that day, of the little clay man. Then I was out the door.

I imagine there may be some of you who remember the name "Joseph Adler." You may have read his memoir, *The Book of Hell*, which I still see from time to time in used bookstores, its black jacket tattered or missing. My father-in-law owns a copy, though he has an extensive library of books on Jewish subjects and owns copies of a lot of books that nobody reads anymore.

I have a copy of my own, one which my father bought right after it came out. It's a well-written, fairly brutal account of the two years the author, a Prague-born Jewish journalist, spent in Theresienstadt. All the usual horrors are present, and although there is an interesting chapter on the secret camp newspaper, *Vadem*, in the end there is nothing really to distinguish the book from any of the many literary memoirs that have been written about those times. The only passage of interest to us here is a brief paragraph that concerns, very much in passing, the Golem of Prague:

> One morning I found myself in possession of five potatoes that were free of rot and not overly endowed with eyes. A man approached me offering to trade for them. In return for my potatoes he said that he would give me the magic tablet, inscribed with secret writing, that had once lain under the tongue of the famous Golem of Prague and was responsible for bringing to life that legendary Jewish automaton. He said that it was a lucky charm and would protect me from evil. We settled on two of my potatoes and went our separate ways. Shortly thereafter, I heard the man had been killed. As for the tablet, incised with Hebrew characters which I was days in trying to make out, it was lost in the disorder that followed my liberation.

Interestingly, one also encounters the Golem of Prague in the pages of *Strangely Enough!*, in a piece entitled "The Phantom of the Synagogue." In it "C. B. Colby" recounts the basic legend of Rabbi Judah's golem—the blood libels, the shaping of the clay of the Moldau River, the need to put an end to the Golem's career, and the persistent rumor that the lifeless form of the Golem still slumbers in the attic of the Alt-Neu Synagogue in Prague's ancient ghetto. Nothing is said, however, about the placing of any magic tablet inscribed with Hebrew letters under the Golem's tongue.

Those of you who lived in and around Washington, D.C. during that time may dimly recall the scandal that followed the book's publication, and a few particulars of the strange case of the writer the *Washington Post* called "The Liar Who Got Lost in His Lie." About six months after the book came out, you may remember, a woman came forward to denounce Joseph Adler, or C. B. Colby. This woman had stumbled upon *The Book of Hell* in her local library and, seeing the author photo, had recognized in the delicate, birdlike features of old Mr. Adler the unmistakable lineaments of a Czech Nazi journalist named Victor Fischer, an admirer and eventual successor of the notorious propagandist Julius Streicher and one of those chiefly responsible for spreading the lie about the ideal conditions to be found in Theresienstadt, where Fischer's accuser had herself been interned.

The Wiesenthal Center took an interest; the *Washington Post* investigated. Mr. Adler denied the woman's claims, hired a lawyer, and promised to fight the charges. Soon afterward, however, he collapsed, and had to be hospitalized. He had suffered a stroke. From his hospital bed, he composed a remarkable statement to the *Post*. I remember reading it to myself one morning over my bowl of Quisp cereal. In his statement, Mr. Adler acknowledged being Victor Fischer and described the destitution and despair into which he had fallen after the war, roaming penniless and starving through the Czech countryside. He described being set upon by a roving gang of Jews bent on murderous revenge, and told how his life had been spared through the kind intercession of a Jewish girl, herself a survivor, whom he eventually married—the late Mrs. Adler. In 1946 he and his new bride had emigrated to the United States, Fischer carrying the passport of a dead Jew, Joseph Adler, whose identity, on his arrival in New York, he eagerly and persuasively assumed. He resumed his journalistic career, writing for a number of newspapers and magazines, and in time came, or so he claimed, to be Joseph Adler. The whole lifelong charade had been pulled off with the knowing connivance of his wife, whose numerical tattoo had served as the model for the one which she herself pricked into his arm with a sewing needle.

Looking back I find that my recollections of the *Book of Hell* business are mingled with and effaced by concurrent memories of the Watergate scandal and with overarching outrage at my parents' divorce. I remember seeing Mr. Adler's statement in the paper, as I've said. I can remember my mother's shock and sense of betrayal by the man she had fed from her own kitchen. But the thing I remember the clearest is the day they came to take Mr. Adler's things away.

Once he entered the hospital, Mr. Adler never returned to the modest blue house on our street. One by one the goldfish in the pond fell prey to the neighborhood cats; then a kind of green pudding appeared on the surface of the water. After a few more months there was nothing in the fishpond but a slick black mat of rotten leaves. And then one day a large Mayflower van pulled up. I happened to be passing by on my bicycle and stopped to watch the burly men carrying out the furniture, the giant twist of barbed wire, the endless boxes of books. There were a lot of crazy sculptures, and the moving men cracked jokes about them and how ugly they were and the things that some people called art. Their harshest humor they reserved, however, for an immense clay statue of a man, taller than any of them and weighing so much that it took three movers to carry it out of the house. It was a crude figure, lumpy and misshapen, with blocky feet and stubby fingers and a wide, impassive face. I recognized it at once: it was the tiny doll that I had glimpsed lying on a glass-and-metal étagère. It had grown, just as golems grew in the legends; as the Golem grew in *Strangely Enough!*, shaped by my great ancestor Rabbi Judah; as a lie grows, ugly and massive as Mr. Adler's lifelong deception, and as heavy as the burden of the guilt and horror that must have driven him so to inhabit and claim as his own the story of a dead Prague Jew.

To this day, I'm not sure what became of Mr. Adler. When I asked my mother recently, she said she thought he had eventually died in a convalescent home. She also remembered having heard sometime afterward that Mr. Adler's original accuser had later recanted, saying she was mistaken in her identification. "I think the woman was actually mentally ill," my mother said. My father, on the other hand, claims that while Mr. Adler may well have been Victor Fischer, he was certainly not C. B. Colby—that C. B. Colby was a well-known journalist and author whose works, many of them on military subjects, were only some of the books that Mr. Adler falsely claimed to have written. All those pseudonyms, according to my father, were actually the real names of writers whom Mr. Adler had chosen to claim to be. As for the golem that I saw them carrying out of his house that day, the three strapping men staggering under its weight as if it were a granite boulder, a chunk of iron fallen from outer space? Well, even if it did exactly resemble the little manikin I'd caught a glimpse of that day as I was leaving his house, then surely the first was a model of the second, a small preliminary work undertaken by the late Mrs. Adler before she began work on the large finished piece.

Now we come, finally, to the Golem of Prague itself. This is the part where things get weird, and I confess to being a little hesitant, having come this far, to press on. The first two golems I've told you about I encountered as a child, and you can blame the things I saw or thought I saw on my youth, and pardon them on the same account, and go along your way secure in the knowledge that stories of golems are myth, folklore, and the hokum of romancers like me. Up to this point, I am not a lunatic or even, necessarily, a liar—except of course to the degree that, professionally, I am both. From here on, however...

It will be recalled that on the day of my uncle Jack's funeral, my father consoled me with one of his standard accounts of our fabulous ancestry, in this case our connection to the great rabbi known as the Maharal, Rabbi Judah ben Loew of Prague. Later, my father would extend this branch laterally, to entangle the popular composer Frederick Loewe, and Marcus Loew, the man who cofounded MGM. For the twenty years that followed, I never had any more evidence to believe or disbelieve his claim of there being some kind of personal connection between me and Rabbi Judah than I did for any of the other claims he made. I grew up, and kept writing. In time, to our mutual regret, I found myself estranged from my father and from the unbelievable things I had once believed about him.

In the meantime, I had begun to publish stories of my own, stories, in some cases, about fathers who disappointed their sons. The fathers in these stories were golem-fathers. I wove alphabetical spells around them, and breathed life into them, and they got up and walked out into the world and caused trouble and embarrassment for the small man of flesh and blood in whose image they had been cast. Or maybe it was I who was the golem, my father's golem, animated by the enchantment of his narratives and lies, then rising up until

I posed a danger to him and all the unlikely things that he, strangely enough, believed in.

Along the way I met a woman, and we decided to get married. She was not a Jew. To us—to the woman in question and me, I mean—this fact did not pose a problem. Of all the relatives of mine then living to whom it might have posed a problem, only the opinion of my grandfather mattered to me. But if he had any reservations about the match on religious grounds, he kept them to himself. Resistance, or at any rate a hint of misgiving, arose from an unexpected quarter: my father, perhaps the least observant self-identified Jew I've ever known, and believe me, that's saying a lot.

He waited to voice his doubts, as has always been his wont in such matters, until the last possible moment, when it was for all practical purposes too late to do anything about them. On the night before the wedding, at the rehearsal dinner, which was held at a French restaurant on Lake Union (I was marrying a Seattleite), he took me aside. His approach was oblique. "You know, you're a *kohen*," he said, meaning a member, by tradition, of the hereditary caste of Jewish high priests, a distinction that supposedly dates back to our forty years spent refusing to stop for directions in the Sinai desert. By now, you can't be too surprised to find my father including us among them. "Right," I said. "Rabbi Judah." "Oh, it goes back much farther than that," he said, and I thought, We're related to Moses himself. But instead of making the expected flight into the genealogical empyrean, my father's face softened, and his eyes grew wistful, and he looked unaccountably sad. "All those generations of Jews marrying Jews," he said. "Thousands and thousands of years of people like your mother and me." "Yeah, well, you and Mom divorced," I said. Oh, I was feeling very cocky. Then it was time for the toasts, and my father turned away from me. Three years from that day the Seattle girl and I would be divorced too.

After we had been married for about a month, and were living in Laguna Beach, a package arrived. In *The Amazing Adventures of Kavalier & Clay* I would employ the powers bestowed on me by Napoleon or my father and transform it into a crate, a massive wooden crate big enough to hold the huge clay man that I had seen them carrying out of Mr. Adler's house that afternoon. In reality it was just a small parcel, about the size of a paperback book—about the size, come to think of it, of *Strangely Enough!* It was wrapped in brown paper, with a pasted-on label that seemed to have been typed on an old manual typewriter. There was no return address. When I opened it I found, wrapped in a wad of cotton batting—can you guess?

It was a small, rough tablet of clay, half as big as a credit card and three times as thick. The clay was dark and worn smooth at the corners. On one side you could make out the traces of some characters—Hebrew letters, I supposed—that had been cut into the surface with a stylus or pin.

At this point, after everything I've told you so far, I expect that you realize at once what the thing was, or what it purported to be. But at the time, years removed from Uncle Jack and Mr. Adler, from golems and my heritage real and imagined, I had no idea what it was supposed to be, only that holding it gave me a strange sense of uneasiness. My then wife and I were graduate students, and some of our friends were artists, and I figured that somebody was having a joke at my expense. My then wife walked in on me as I was staring at it, and before I could think about what I was doing, I threw the tablet into the trash, along with the junk mail and circulars from Thrifty Drug. For some reason I didn't want her to see it.

About two years later, we had moved, trying to outrun the doom that was on us. We were living up in Puget Sound, on an island. It was a beautiful place, but I think I may have been, at the time, the only Jew living there; that, at any rate, was how I felt. One day when I drove into town to check our mailbox at the P.O., I found another small parcel awaiting me. It contained another small tablet. Actually, though I knew it was impossible, it seemed to be the same tablet, only this time the letters were so effaced as to be no more than scratches, nicks in the thing's dusty surface. I had given no thought to that other mysterious gift since throwing it away in Laguna Beach, but I had been giving increasing thought—furtively, secretly, lying awake in the middle of the night with my goyish wife sleeping beside me—to my father's words at the rehearsal dinner. The subject of children was beginning to come up, more and more insistently as my wife got older, and somehow, magically, every time it did we ended up having a painful, sticky, difficult argument—about *religion!* A subject I had never argued about with anybody in my life before! How can you tell me it's important for our children to be Jewish, she would say with perfect justification, when it doesn't seem to be at all important to you?

This time I recognized the tablet for what it was: a magic tablet for animating a golem, to be placed under its tongue by the hand of an adept. A reminder of Mr. Adler and his wishful lies, of the place where he claimed to have suffered. A reminder of all those who truly had died there, or at the next evil stop down the line. A reminder of all those generations of Jews, circling one another under the marriage canopy, intoning their spells, in order to bring into existence a golem, me, the embodiment of an ancient and simple wish: let there be more of us. Let us not disappear. I wondered who could have sent it—if perhaps old

Mr. Adler was out there somewhere, busily forging magic tablets and keeping track of my whereabouts. Or perhaps the culprit was my father. In any case, this time—my heart, my conscience, my thoughts weighed down by the golem-heavy burden of memory—I put the thing in my pocket. I carried it there as the marriage dissolved. I was carrying it when I met my present wife, Ayelet, herself the product of generations of Jews marrying Jews and no doubt, though my father has never said anything about it, a third cousin three times removed.

Brother, you're thinking. All this nattering on about golems and wishes and lies, and in the end the point comes down to one of your own kind, stick to your own kind. But that isn't the point. I don't know what the point is. All I know is that one sunny afternoon, not long after we met, I found myself in Jerusalem with Ayelet, at Yad Vashem, the Israeli national museum of the Shoah, or Holocaust, and my heart was broken. I came out into the sunshine and burst into tears and just stood there, crying, and the weight of the thing I carried, that tablet compounded of wishes and lies, that five-thousand-year burden of mothers and fathers and the wondrous, bitter story of their lives, almost knocked me down.

Our next stop before coming home was, of all places, Prague. Duly we made our way down to the ghetto, or what's left of it, and trooped around the old Jewish cemetery, with it snaggled headstones lying like teeth in a jawbone. That's where they buried old Rabbi Judah, and his grave is now a kind of pilgrimage site, strewn with memorial stones and penciled notes and withered flowers.

I knelt down beside the grave there, and in a patch of dirt I formed the hasty outline of a man. Where his mouth would be I opened a hole, and worked the clay tablet down into it. Then I took Ayelet's hand in mine and walked away.

I haven't received another one since, though I'm still looking out for it in the mail. I'm still listening to my father, too, and wishing as he wished—as we all wish, Jews and non-Jews alike—to be part of something ancient and honorable and greater than myself. And, naturally, I'm still telling lies.

POSTSCRIPT, AUGUST 2007

The preceding is the text of a talk that I delivered publicly several times over the course of 2003–04. Its subject is the interrelationship between truth and lies, memory and invention, history and story, memoir and fiction, the sources of narrative and the storytelling impulse; the inevitable fate of liars to be swallowed up or crushed by their lies; and the risks inherent both in discounting the power of outright fiction to reveal the truths of a life, and in taking at face value the fictions that writers of memoir present as fact. The matter struck me (some three years before the exposures of J. T. Leroy and James Frey) as valid and important but hardly novel or surprising, and rather than deal with it in a straightforward expository manner, for my talk I elected to put on a kind of demonstration. Instead of just making commonplace assertions like "writers of fiction are professional liars" or "there is a kinship between lies and stories," I wanted to try to show an audience just how tangled the interrelationship can be. I was hoping, mostly, that it might be more fun that way, for audiences and for me.

So I crafted a narrative in the form of a memoir, one constructed partly from the materials of my actual biography—my having lived in Flushing in 1968, grown up in Columbia, Maryland with a father given to the cultivation of what Freud called "family romance," loved a book called *Strangely Enough!* by C. B. Colby, married a woman (my first wife) who was not Jewish—and partly from pure invention. This is, of course, a technique common both to liars and writers of fiction: to give credibility to invented details by blending them with factual ones.

This talk was written to be performed, and in writing and performing it I was always conscious of my audience. It has often been observed that the writing of fiction is akin to the work of a stage magician, a feat of sustained deception in which by imagery and language the trickster leads the audience to believe in the existence or possibility of a series of nonexistent or impossible things. In fiction and in stage magic, one result of this deception, if it works, is the experience of pleasure in the audience at the verisimilitude of the effect. In both cases the pleasure is possible—indeed, it depends entirely—on the audience's knowing perfectly well that it is being fooled, on its avid willingness to be fooled, to participate in creating the illusion of reality. This, of course, is the essential difference between fiction and lies. There is a contract between the writer of fiction and the readers he or she lies to, as there is between a magician and the audience he hoodwinks; they are in it together. They are helping each other to bring a story to apparent life or an edible orange to grow from the branch of a clockwork tree.

It was never, in giving this talk, my hope to make people actually believe that I had, for example, once known a Holocaust survivor who passed himself off as a writer, but who then turned out to be a different writer who was passing himself off as a Holocaust survivor who had himself been a writer, with all of the progress of this ever-widening gyre of lies marked and measured by the growth of a clay homunculus to prodigious size. The possibility that somebody would believe or even half believe the semipreposterous tale never occurred to me; but making somebody believe it wasn't even remotely the point. The point was to try to tangle and disentangle and tangle again the lines of truth and fiction before the audience's very eyes, so to speak, and let them feel (or so I hoped) the excitement that comes from handling the raw materials of golem-craft, of bringing inanimate facts of clay, through imagination and invention, to a fabulous kind of life.

Magicians have different ways of acknowledging, while performing their tricks, that they are tricks. That's part of the fun. They tell the audience that they are going to be fooled, and they challenge the audience to spot the mechanism, to see through the deception. Or they guarantee that all the marvels the audience is about to see are verifiable feats of magic, and insist, deadpan, that the lady has in fact been sawed in two. Or they pile it on, using grandiose language, hyperbolic and preposterous claims about the provenance and genuineness of the tricks in their repertoire. All of these are ways of engaging the audience to maintain and participate in the deception.

Beginning with its dubious title, and throughout the talk, I engaged in the fiction writer's versions of these magical strategies. I repeatedly—to the point of absurdity—insisted on the truth of everything that I was saying, no matter how ridiculous, impossible, unlikely, or strange. Indeed it was usually at the most unbelievable moments in the story that I made such assertions. I also employed the common magician's device of asking the audience to assent to a premise that I had not bothered to demonstrate or prove, telling them, for instance, that some of them might remember the case of my fictitious liar, Joseph Adler, from reading about it in the newspaper. Once I even took from my pocket a small chunk of brown brick I had found in the parking lot outside the lecture hall, brandished it, and claimed that it was the lost toe of the Golem of Flushing; but afterward I lost it and never repeated this particular flourish.

Furthermore I employed a number of nonverbal cues in the course of the performance to signal my intentions to the audience. As a friend who attended my talk in Seattle wrote to me, "Pursuing all this on the page really leaves out a huge part of the performance—your timing, your facial expressions, your body language. It's funny, but those are the elements I remember most."

My sense, in giving the talk all over the country to diverse audiences of literate, intelligent, engaged people, was that the talk was taken exactly in the spirit in which I intended it. They understood that it was not a "real" memoir but an avowedly fictional one, right up to the very last word, and I think that almost everyone understood the literary arguments in the service of which the fictional memoir had been offered. I make this assertion on the basis of the audience reaction as I perceived it during the course of the talks, and on the comments that people made to me afterward. A typical remark was something like "That part about writing the story about Sherlock Holmes and Captain Nemo was true, though, right?" or "I know the part about you living on Vashon Island is true!" When people said things like this, I would laugh and say something like "Are you saying you didn't believe the rest of it? I'm outraged!" or "What do you mean *that* part was true?" I was teasing them, in a very obvious way. There was so much about the talk and my style of delivering it that was obvious, sometimes I worried I was hamming it up too much.

Nonetheless, there were people who did not seem to catch on entirely. There is no denying that. I believe that there were not very many such people. But there were a few who came up to me after the talk was over, and asked me about Joseph Adler, or the location of the candy store that I had said my uncle had owned in Harlem, or even about my claims of having seen golems. I will confess that, at first, I felt a mild sense of exhilaration when this occurred. If you made a man out of clay, and it really did get up and walk around, you would probably feel the same way—at first. But shortly thereafter you would begin to feel uneasy, and that is what I came to feel when somebody—and of course it really didn't happen very often—asked me about Joseph Adler.

I'd had a similar experience with *The Amazing Adventures of Kavalier & Clay*. To my surprise, I discovered that there were readers who came away from the novel believing that Sam Clay and Joe Kavalier had really existed, that they had really created a character known as the Escapist back in the '40s, and that somewhere out there you would be able to find and purchase old Escapist comic books and perhaps even original artwork drawn by Joe Kavalier. These people wrote me letters and emails asking me how they could obtain such things. I confess that I tended to view people like this as having a certain amount of the sucker in them. I was not looking for suckers. God knows I was not trying to sucker anybody. But the suckers are out there, and they will get suckered whether you want them to or not.

On the signing line after the first public reading I did from my novel *The Yiddish Policemen's Union*, which presents among other deceptions an entirely fictitious, entirely Jewish modern-day city of Sitka, Alaska, an apparently intelligent and literate woman approached me to say that she had been to Sitka on a cruise and was astonished to learn now that she had somehow missed seeing all of those Jews up there. She didn't remember any of the tall buildings either. She was not challenging me on my facts, and she was not joking. She was simply wonderstruck by her own failure to have seen all of that from the deck of her cruise ship. Listening to me read the first chapter of my novel—fully advertised as such by me in my opening remarks—was enough to make her doubt her own recollections, to accept my sophisticated lie over the crude but veracious fragments of her own memory.

I felt that Trickster flush of surprise, triumph, satisfaction: *Sucker!* It made me giddy; it also made me feel a little ill. I didn't know how to disabuse her, or whether I ought to do so at all. On the one hand, I had indeed been trying, at the most fundamental level, to deceive her, along with every reader the novel would ever find, into the most passionate and foolish belief. But at the same time I was also trying, always, with no greater hope or ambition, to tell her the truth, a truth: to convey my understanding of, my own bit of information on, the nature of Jews and Alaska and Life. It is along the knife-narrow borderland between those two kingdoms, between the Empire of Lies and the Republic of Truth, more than along any other frontier on the map of existence, that Trickster makes his wandering way, and either comes to grief or finds his supper, his treasure, his fate.

"Maybe next time you're there," I told the lady before I signed my name across the title page of another pack of lies. "Check it out."

PROCEEDS FROM THIS BOOK BENEFIT
826 NATIONAL

826 National is an innovative tutoring, writing, and publishing nonprofit based in seven cities across the country. Since opening 826 Valencia, our San Francisco center, in 2002, our goal has been to assist students ages 6-18 with their writing skills while helping teachers get their classes excited about the writing. Our mission is based on the understanding that great leaps in learning can happen with one-on-one attention, and that strong writing skills are fundamental to future success. Due to overwhelming interest from others around the country, 826 Valencia now also serves as the headquarters of 826 National, a tutoring and mentorship model that has been duplicated in six other cities: New York, Los Angeles, Ann Arbor, Chicago, Seattle, and Boston.

Through volunteer support, each of the seven 826 chapters provides drop-in tutoring, class field trips, writing workshops, and in-schools programs—all free of charge—for students, classes, and schools. 826 centers are especially committed to supporting teachers, offering services and resources for English Language Learners, and publishing student work. 826 programming reaches students at every opportunity—in school, after school, in the evenings, and on weekends. Each of the 826 National chapters works to produce professional-quality publications written entirely by young people, to forge relationships with teachers in order to create innovative workshops and lesson plans, to inspire students to write and appreciate the written word, and to rally thousands of enthusiastic volunteers to make it all happen. By offering all of our programming for free, we aim to serve families who cannot afford to pay for the level of personalized instruction their children receive through 826 chapters.

The demand for 826 National's services is tremendous. Last year we worked with more than 4,000 volunteers and over 18,000 students nationally, hosted 368 field trips, completed 170 major in-schools projects, offered 266 evening and weekend workshops, welcomed over 130 students per day for after-school tutoring, and produced over 600 student publications. At many of our centers, our field trips are fully booked almost a year in advance, teacher requests for in-school tutor support continue to rise, and the majority of our evening and weekend workshops have waitlists.

826 National volunteers are local community residents—professional writers, teachers, artists, college students, parents, bankers, lawyers, and retirees from a wide range of professions. These passionate individuals can be found at all of our centers after school, sitting side-by-side with our students, providing one-on-one attention. They can be found running our field trips, or helping an entire classroom of local students learn how to write a story, or assisting student writers during one of our Young Authors' Book Programs. All day and in a variety of ways, our volunteers are actively connecting with youth from the communities we serve.

TO LEARN MORE OR GET INVOLVED, PLEASE VISIT
WWW.826NATIONAL.ORG

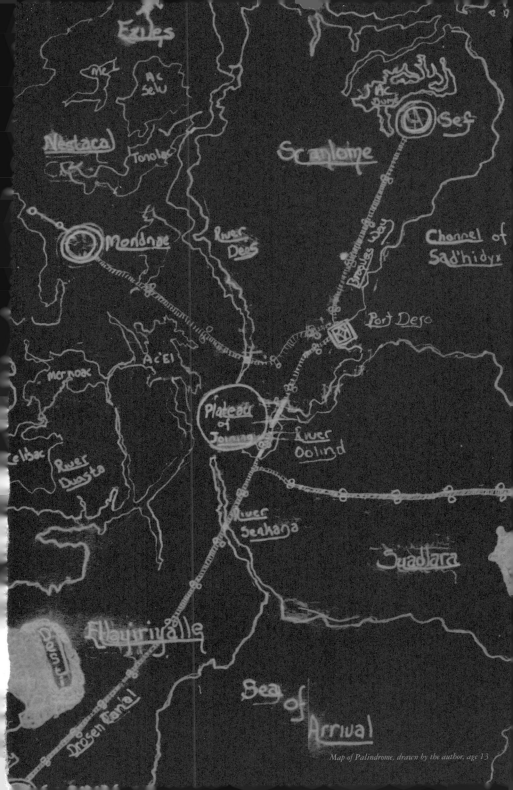

Map of Palindrome, drawn by the author, age 13